Reflections On My Own Mortality
My Battle With The Big C

3

Table of contents

Part 1
   Before Chemotherapy

Part 2
   The Calm Before The Storm

Part 3
   My Journey Begins

Part 4
   My Journey Comes To An End

Reflections On My Own Mortality
My Battle With The Big C

For Philip
I never gave up.

Part 1
Before Chemotherapy

ONE

It's really ironic, isn't it, how we spend our youth tossing caution to the wind at every turn, believing we will live forever?

I know I did.

I think we all do, when we are growing up. I grew up in the baby boomer generation, for example, and the only cares we had was going to school, riding our bikes around the neighborhood until dark, going home to eat dinner at the family table, then TV and bedtime.

Then, on weekends, we'd be up early, eating a bowl of cereal and watching Saturday morning cartoons, then out to meet up with our friends for a long day of creating new adventures, and some more great memories, of course.

We all unknowingly took it all for granted, never having any inclination that we'd grow older by the day, month, and year. Graduating from highschool, getting a job, starting a family.

Growing up.

The whole time, as we moved on, growing older and hopefully wiser and happier, never having any idea that someday, whether it be a few years from now or decades from now, we would eventually have to face our own mortality.

In my case, it was in the form of a cancer, that

invaded my lymphnodes, and moved on to my chest.

It's funny – well, ironic, that is – how your own mortality tends to show you just how *vulnerable* you really are, and at a time when you thought that your life was going pretty well, despite your other recent disappointments – and heartaches.

When the old grim reaper came to visit me – in the form of squamous cell carcinoma – I had just gone through the death my beloved cat, Toby, my best friend friend from gradeschool, Phil, and my mother, who had spent the last two years in a nursing home until she had mercifully passed away in her sleep.

My mind, heart, and soul had already been torn asunder, and I was just barely getting back into the swing of things when my body began to betray me in the form of the "Big C."

#

I had begun with a simple sore throat and a cough, with the cough being a bit more persistent than the soreness in my throat. In the past, these symptoms, for me, had been merely signs my sinus trouble was flaring up because of a change in the weather, so I simply purchased some over the counter medicine and thought no more of it.

A few weeks later, my cough had subsided, but my sore throat was becoming almost unbearable.

Then one night, as I stood in front of the bathroom mirror brushing my teeth, I saw it; a very small but visible lump under my tongue, and a small but visible lump on the right side of my throat.

I knew then that sinus trouble was going to be the least of my worries in the future.

TWO

Over the next few weeks, I spent countless bours at the doctor's office or the hospital, undergoing countless tests and exams and being poked and prodded and given certain medications and having x-rays and pet scans, and well...you name it, I had been subjected to it.

Now, bear in mind, this was during the same time I had just been diagnosed with an enlarged prostate, high blood pressure, as well as cataracts in both eyes, so the thought of possibly having cancer wasn't exactly what someone in my shoes wanted to deal with.

Then, of all things that could have happened to me, the pain intensified.

#

I don't know if you have ever experienced the degree of pain that swollen, cancerous lymphnodes can produce, but if not, I hope and pray you *never* have to go through this. I wouldn't wish this kind of pain and discomfort on my worst enemy – that is, if I had one. These days, I do my best to let bygones be just that, in the past, and love more than hate.

I thought I'd felt extreme pain in the past, but there was absolutely *no* comparison.

I'd had my left thumb crushed off at work and

grafted back on, had twenty-eight teeth pulled {a lot of them having been infected} had a broken nose, black eyes, kicked in the groin, I mean...I had experienced all sorts of pain, but nothing like the pain I experienced with what I not so fondly refer to as "The Big C."

#

It began slowly, like a nocturnal predator slithering through the darkness, sneaking up on me, bit by bit, just a little worse each day, until the day that over the counter pain relievers no longer had any effect at all, except for providing me with acid reflux and an upset stomach.

By that time, the pain in my throat was so extreme, I couldn't eat or drink anything without being in pain. My diet began to change, and rapid weight loss followed, to add insult to injury.

My doctor quickly prescribed some very powerful pain meds he referred to as "Norco," and since then, at least I have something to combat the pain with at times it becomes too overbearing.

But...then I had the "side effects" of my new medication to deal with; chronic constipation, stomach cramps, and acid reflux.

Back to the doctor again!

THREE

Just when I thought I'd seen it all as far as pain or discomfort was concerned, then came the rapid and not so subtle changes in my daily life style.

Where as I had been used to the same sleeping schedule, working on my computer each day at a certain time, eating at a certain time, etc.

But not after the Big C had grabbed ahold of me and turned my life upside down.

#

One thing about the Big C, it isn't prejudice. In it's beady little evil eyes, we are *all* equally worthless and subject to extreme bodily pain and psychological torture.

It isn't concerned with skin color or personal background or what Church you attend – or don't bother attending – on Sunday mornings.

All it is concerned with is making your life as miserable {and maybe as short} as possible, and as quickly as possible.

Then there are the *dreams*.

#

Well, more like nightmares, actually.

You combine your current state of health, your daily meds and other supplements, your narcotic pain relievers, and, of course, your current frame of mind, if you *are* lucky enough to go to sleep, it will be a fitful sleep at best.

My sleep patterns have changed a lot since my diagnosis; instead of falling asleep within a reasonable amount of time, I now lay there wide awake, my mind always racing with ghastly visions of the cancer inside of me, moving around again, the tiny little evil cells coarsing through my bloodstream, attacking everything in sight.

One night, I had a dream that my cancer was actually chasing me, and was catching up to me, when, suddenly, I was whisked away into a bright light up in the clouds, which I'm sure was Heaven.

Then I woke up to the same old thing I always wake up to; sleep deprevation, headache, sour stomach, and fatigue.

I still think it ws Heaven I saw, though. At least I hope it was.

#

That's another thing about cancer you can always depend on; it will test your faith.

I'm not necessarily talking about your faith in God, either. I'm speaking, in general, of one's faith in *themselves*.

In my situation, if you didn't try your best to have faith in *yourself*, to carry on as best you can, no matter what life tossed at you on any given day, you just...*give up*, believe me, you *will die*, and possibly sooner than later.

You have to remain positive. You have to remain calm. You have to do your best to live each and every day as though it may be your last, but, at the same time, you must also keep the *faith*, the faith that God graced you with upon birth, that you *will* make it through all of this someday.

Without your faith, and faith in yourself, you might as well roll back over in the morning and give up.

I, myself, don't intend to do so.

FOUR

It always strikes me as really amusing – but not in a cruel, uncaring way, of course – how tough some guys think they are until the Big C pays them a visit.

I used to think I was a real tough guy, too. I mean, in the way of being gifted with a strong constitution for hard work, and a threshold for pain. I had inherited that from my Father, James, and I was gifted with a good, kind heart from my Mother, Jeanne.

But, you toss cancer into the mix, and even the toughest of guys can end up a blubbering mess.

I remember the day I was told I had cancer. I sat there, taking it all in, pretending to be a tough guy. Then, when I got home, in private, I sat down in my room and cried like a baby with a dirty diaper.

Tough guy...yeah, *right*.

#

But don't worry, guys, it doesn't make you *weak* to break down and cry.

It doesn't make you any less of a man, It doesn't make you appear childish in front of your loved ones. It doesn't make you look like a big baby in front of your friends.

It shows that you have a big heart, a *good* heart,

and, last, but not least, it shows that you are man enough to know when you are defeated.

But, what do we do when we are defeated?

We get back up, brush ourselves off, and jump right back into the fight again,

It works the same way with cancer.

You know you have a *very* formidable opponent you're dealing with, and you know you have to fight the toughest fight you've ever fought in your life if you are to survive.

You can do it.

I know.

#

You may wake up in the morning feeling even weaker and more fatigued that the day before. You may look in the bathroom mirror at those weak, bloodshot eyes and pale skin and thinning hair, and wonder how you're going to make it through.

You may fall asleep at night wondering if you will even wake up in the morning. Or if you will wake up feeling even worse.

You may wake up sick at your stomach and weak in the knees and barely make it into the bathroom before voiding your stomach of all or any nutritional content you may have had stored there.

You may find yourself curled up on the floor and crying and wishing it was all over, even if it meant that you just...*gave up*.

I don't think anyone could blame you.

Even God.

But, that means you lost your *faith*, and let yourself down.

When you needed yourself and your strength the most.

So you crawl back to your bed, take a short nap, and while you're lying there, you promise yourself – and God – that the next day, you will *not* let this beat you down.

You are *still* a tough guy.

If you were *not* a tough guy, you wouldn't be so bound and determined to fight the Big C with all your heart and soul now, would you?

Just saying.

FIVE

What has really amazed me about my journey so far, is my own willpower.

You'd really be surprised how the word "cancer" tends to make a guy wake up and smell the roses, so to speak.

I wake up each day, knowing that those nasty little cancer cells are most likely migrating further down South, but still do my level best to enjoy my day.

Dealing with the Big C, a lot of the process is *psychological*, you know. Seriously.

It's in your own personal mindset on certain days. For example, if you wake up feeling really low down? If the weather permits? Take a walk around the neighborhood. Chat with your neighbors.

Literally *stop* and smell the roses.

Stop and pet the neighborhood cats.

Listen to the birdies sing.

Gaze up at the sunshine and fluffy white clouds and be thankful for the opportunity.

Or, just in case you aren't feeling up to any outdoor activities, find something you enjoy doing on the *inside*.

Watch your favorite TV show.

Eat one of your favorite snacks.

Order a pizza and watch a DVD.

Read a good book.

Enjoy one of your favorite hobbies.

If you don't have any particular hobbies, take up a *new* hobby.

You get the idea.

Do *not* allow the Big C to run your life for you; *you* run your *own* life.

Stop, take a deep breath, close your eyes, and use your *willpower* to overcome the moment in a *positive* way. *Positive* thoughts.

You can do it. Believe me, I know.

#

But, if you are having one of these really bad days, and your willpower isn't quite up to par, keep this in mind:

God and Jesus are rooting for you. God's plan for you is not over yet. If this was meant to be your *last* days on this beautiful Earth God created for us, you wouldn't be here to live yet another day.

You *can* do it. Just open your heart to God and keep telling yourself...*I can do this*.

Your journey, just like mine, isn't quite over yet. Keep the faith and *BELIEVE*.

SIX

Recently, I have even found cancer to be inspirational.

I mean, what else could make you want to get up in the morning early to take care of business, when you wake up feeling like you've been run over by a train?

I wake up almost every day feeling like I've been rode hard and hung up wet, but as soon as my cell phone alarm goes off {The theme from *the X-Files* TV show} I'm up and ready to face the world.

Well, almost, anyway. But in my position, almost is definitely better than nothing. Because you know, by now, if you do *not* get your butt up out of bed, you'll most likely just lay there and never want to get out of bed, unless it's to use the bathroom {that is, unless you are armed with a pair of Depends} or grab a bite to eat, and spend the rest of your day laying in bed feeling sorry for yourself.

So...yes, cancer, for me, has become *very* inspirational to say the least.

#

As a writer – and as most other fellow writers know from experience – there really *is* such a thing as writer's block.

It does happen.

But, you toss in a good dose of the Big C into your daily routine, and a case of writer's block can be come darn near debilitating.

That's just one more reason I try my best to to use my current situation as a *gift*, an inspiration, that should be kept in tow at all costs, to be preserved and nurtured.

As a writer – and as most fellow writers know – something this precious is a gift from God, and he didn't bestow this gift upon you just to watch you allow it to wither away.

Yes, the Big C has been an inspiration for my writing, indeed.

#

Speaking of inspiration, my kitty cat, Holly Jean, has most definitely been another valuable source of inspiration for me since this all began.

Don't get me wrong; she has always been a valauble source of love and happiness and companionship. It's just that after I found out I had cancer, she really stepped up to bat, so to speak.

Believe me, your fur babies *know* when you're sick.

Since my diagnosis – the exact *day* of my diagnosis, as a matter of fact - Holly Jean has been by my side day and night. She is either sitting on my lap or by my chair or sleeping with me at night, all snuggled up with me, keeping me warm and purring up a storm.

They *KNOW,* and do their best to make their owner feel loved and appreciated and safe and warm, just like their owner did for them, in giving them a forever home.

Believe me, Holly Jean has paid me back in *Spades*. Not that I expected her to do so, but she has.

What more could I ask for?

Yes, my Holly Jean has been an inspiration, indeed.

SEVEN

But, unfortunately, there are still days, like this one, that all of the inspiration in the world can't make you feel too inspired.

As I sit here today, at my trusty old Acer laptop, typing away, I'm doing so in a lot of pain and discomfort, my unwanted guest, Mr Big C, bound and determined to cripple my inspiration at every turn.

Over the last several days – between November the third and November the sixth – the pain in my throat, in my lymphnodes, has grown almost intolerable in it's intensity.

It feels as though the pain – the cancer itself – is slowly but surely trying to wrap itself around my entire skull, squeezing and crushing it.

My lower right jaw feels like it's beginning to fracture, come loose, and the pain is moving up the right side of my skull to the back of my head, the pressure almost unbearable.

At times, it feels as though the pain behind my eyes will cause them to literally burst forth from the sockets, and my vision gets blurry.

It is times like these that I am in dire need of further inspiration – and faith – to get through this for yet another day, so, I pop another Norco pill, sit back down at my computer, and start writing again.

It's all I have right now.

#

It's better than nothing.

For me, to be able to sit down at my computer and type away and create something new – like *this* story, a *true* story, one of self awareness and hope and faith and love and determination, for future generations of cancer patients and survivors to read – was all worth it in the end, no matter how things turn out for me.

But I do hope I'm still around at the end of this journey, not out of selfishness, mind you, but just to prove that my self determination, willpower, and most of all my faith, got me through, and I beat the Big C at it's own wicked game.

Therefore, I write.

#

Sometimes, I sit back and wonder, is cancer actually some form of punishment?

I mean, one from God?

Not to say that our God is an unkind or uncaring God, one without love or compassion for his many children. But, in the grand scheme of things, could cancer be a way to punish those of us who spent too much time taking our blessings for granted, and now, the cancer is way for those to prove themselves, redeem themselves, prove their worth in the eyes of God?

Prove their love and faith for their almighty,

loving, and forgiving God?
	I guess I'll find out soon enough.

Part 2
The Calm Before The Storm

EIGHT

Only nine days left until chemo, and all of the lovely side effects I'm sure will come with it.

By now, whereas before I could handle the pressure this situation has bestowed upon me, today, November the tenth, 2023, I'm slowly but surely beginning to lose my composure.

With each day that goes by, I become more stressed out and depressed, suffering from sleep deprivation, and loss of appetite.

But, each day, I get up, get motivated, and do my level best to carry on with my usual routine.

That's because I have no other choice.

#

Remember what I said about cancer being inspirational?

Well, it can be, but by this point in my journey, it has also become a constant, relentless irritant, one that almost seems like it has a life of it's own – which in reality it does – and the only thing missing is the damn stuff actually *speaking* to me.

Oh yes...I'm still here, and I will be here all the way to the end, to see you fail, and watch you fall. You had best hold that so called "faith" of yours close, because you are going to need it.

Oh, don't worry, I *will*.

#

I have never been one to lose the faith, but lately, I'll have to admit, I've come close.

Not that I've lost faith in God, mind you, but in myself, to pull this off. I've never been suicidal, either, but I'll have to admit, lately, I've found myself wondering if I might be better off giving up and giving in, just admit to myself that all of this pain and misery just might not be worth the fight.

It's not being weak or spineless, either. It's not that you aren't a tough guy anymore.

It's called being *human*.

A mere mortal experiencing a temporary moment of weakness, and nothing more.

Now...back to writing my story.

NINE

There has been one bright spot in all of this {other than my brother and my kitty being there for me} in the form of yet another guardian angel, a lovely lady named Kerri Pruitt, my onocology advocate at GSH.

She has been there all along, every day, keeping up with me in the middle of her busy day, making sure that I had everything I needed, and to answer any burning questions I may have about my upcoming treatment.

She has put up with my sudden outbursts of anger over my current situation and tried to keep me calm. She has made important phone calls for me when my throat hurt too much to talk to anyone. She has supplied me with a nice binder full of important information that will be relevant to my procedures and how to prepare for them.

She always has a big smile on her face and a great personality and makes you feel calm and safe in her hands.

She is a real credit to her profession and to all of her patients as well.

I look upon her as my "calm before the storm," so to speak, the bright spot in the distance in the middle of the storm, that will be there to keep me afloat if my boat begins to sink beneath the waves in the storm known as cancer.

What more could I ask for?

#

So, I sit here and write my story.

It's all I can do.

I have to *finish* my story, because that will mean I *beat* cancer – at least long enough to finish my story, that is – which would be a miracle in itself.

Maybe, just *maybe*, deep down inside, that's what I'm *really* hoping for; a miracle. If so, that's just fine, too. Who couldn't use a good old fashioned miracle now and then?

I know I could.

A good old fashioned miracle, in the midst of the storm, some more calm in the midst of all this irrationality, some peace of mind most graciously offered up by our almighty God.

So...I keep writing my story.

TEN

Eight days before chemo.

I am sitting here at my computer, working on my story {as you can see} and doing my best to concentrate.

I have been thinking about ways to help me relax and concentrate while I work, and it suddenly came to me, I have always liked music. So, being a member of the baby boomer generation, I look through my assortment of 60s and 70s music; Pink Floyd, The Beatles, The Doors...and, my favorite, The Rolling Stones.

The Stones it is.

As I listen to the all too distinctive voice of Mick Jagger telling me *he can't get no satisfaction*, it's back to work on my story.

#

I've always been fond of movies too, so I glanced through my DVD collection, Finding several movies I knew I'd enjoy, as well as remembering I had Netflix on my current TV package, I thought I would have a wide variety to choose from indefinitely.

But, the novelty wore off fast.

As always, that deep rooted, ever present,

ominous feeling of *dread*, that underlying *fear*, kicked in again, an all too unpleasant reminder of what lies ahead for me soon enough.

The fear that *Murphy's Law* will take effect, and whatever could go wrong most likely will.

What if the chemo doesn't work?

If not, what treatment will I have to endure next?

Will it be painful? Will I be bedridden?

How LONG will I have to live?

The very thought of myself lying in my bed, unable to help myself, was terrifying to say the least.

Who would take care of me? I can't afford a private nurse. My brother, God bless his soul, would be willing to help me, but he is even older than I am, and has his own health concerns to worry about.

Will I be able to shower by myself? Eat by myself? Go to the bathroom by myself?

Will I even WANT to survive this?

So many feelings, emotions, so many questions and so few real answers.

So...I take a deep breath, exhale, and go back to what I know now I *must* do; work on my story.

ELEVEN

Eight days until chemo.

Still sitting here at my trusty old Acer laptop, typing away, doing my best to concentrate, and listening to Mick Jagger singing about *Jumping Jack Flash He's A Gas Gas Gas!*

Suddenly feeling like I'm more in the mood for some classic Pink Floyd, so I insert *The Wall* CD into my PC, put my headphones on, turn the volume up, and listen to David Gilmour singing about being *comfortably numb*.

I suddenly find that I, *myself*, wish I was also comfortably numb, so I didn't have to feel this all too familiar and almost debilitating pain now surging through my throat and up into my skull.

I am...comfortably numb...

I wish.

#

So, I take another Norco pill.

It's really amazing, isn't it? I mean, how one little white pill, dissolving in my belly, coarsing through my blood stream, can bring about such a feeling of euphoria, of salvation?

Salvation from constant pain and misery. From a

sour stomach and headaches, that would make a migraine headache seem almost mild in comparison.

But as always, it is only a temporary solution to a possibly permanent problem.

Hold on! That little voice in my head tells me. The same little voice that used to tell me it was okay to do naughty stuff when I was a kid. Or to take another drink from a bottle of cheap liquor. Or to smoke another cigarette.

But today, that little voice was trying to help me. *Hold on! Keep the faith! Don't give up now!*

So...I take another deep breath, exhale, and begin typing again.

My story.

My battle with the Big C.

My destiny?

I guess I'll find out soon enough.

But, for now, I must keep writing.

#

I stop briefly to eat a small bowl of cream of wheat, and take some more of my daily meds and vitamin supplements.

It's really amazng how much a person's diet can change after you've been diagnosed with cancer, too.

Whereas I used to eat just about anything I wanted to, junk food, takeout, ice cream, donuts, etc., my daily menu now consists of more health conscious foods; hot cereal, eggs, cottage cheese, yogurt, and low fat milk just to name a few.

I have already figured out that if I toss caution to the wind, eat or drink whatever suits my fancy at the time, once chemo begins, my body will almost immediately *reject* it, and not only make me even sicker than before, but even serve as *fuel* for the cancer.

Note to myself; sugar *fuels* cancer cells. So, no more ice cream sandwiches or milkshakes or gigantic chocolate bars, and absolutely *no sugar* on your breakfast cereal.

Salty or greasy foods? The same thing applies to them, too. Might as well swallow a nice big mouthful of anthrax.

No thanks.

On with my story...

TWELVE

Six days until chemo.

To add insult to injury – as if I really needed that in my life right now – I have been feeling guilty.

Yes, *guilty.*

Why, you ask?

It's simple enough, really, All you need to have in your possession to understand my feeling of guilt is two things; a good heart, and cancer.

You see, I know that it is *my* fault that I have this cancer; too many years of not appreciating the good things I had, and spending way too much time destroying them – although unwittingly – until it was too late to turn back the clock.

I had stopped drinking alcohol in 2007, which of course was a good thing, but kept partaking in the one vice that that would end up giving me cancer, cigarettes.

The guilt of what I have done to myself is bad enough, but what it may do to others is far worse.

#

I'm speaking, of course, of the guilt I am feeling about my family and other loved ones having to sit back and watch me suffer, and worry about me.

They don't deserve to go through this, just because of my own self destructive behavior and selfishness. It isn't fair to them to watch me suffer and be in constant pain – and maybe even *die*.

What an epitaph to leave behind for my kids and grandkids, too.

Mommy, what happened to grandpa? Well, he smoked two packs of cigarettes a day even though the doctors told to stop smoking, and he got this stuff called cancer that killed him. But why didn't he stop? Well, I guess he just didn't CARE enough to stop.

See my point?

How could I *not* feel guilty?

So...I write my story, in hope that they will somehow find it in their heart to forgive me.

#

Another thing that has been weighing heavily on my mind lately is wondering about whether my sweet mother can actually look down upon me from Heaven, and see how I'm suffering.

In a way, I hope she can, so she can pray for me, send me hugs and kisses and be my guardian angel. Believe me, in my position, you can use all the Heavenly hugs and kisses and prayers you can get.

I miss my mother so much right now; her hugs and sweet little kisses on my cheek and telling me, *don't worry, honey, everything will be okay.*

I know words are just that, *words*, but depending on *who* they come from, at a time you really need to hear them, those simple words can mean more than all of the material, Earthly possessions anyone could ever ask for.

You don't take *anything* with you when you die, always remember that.

All of the things you held so dear to your heart, whether it be money, expensive clothing, jewelry, or in my case, cigarettes, it's all left behind when you take that last breath.

I finally realize that now.

I love and miss you so much, Mama. I'm so glad you finally found your peace.

Now, if I can just find my *own*.

THIRTEEN

Still six days until chemo.

I ate my bland but healthy breakfast, have taken my morning meds {including my new best friend, my Norco pill!} and now back to my story.

I'm feeling a little rougher than yesterday. The swelling in my throat is getting worse, and my head feels like it's going explode any second, like an overripe melon.

But what else is new, I guess.

As I type away, I take occasional glances at the small TV set in my office. I am watching a DVD of the old *Twilight Zone* series today, more classic TV from long ago, back when there were still family friendly shows for us to watch.

Don't make em' like that anymore, no sir.

As I steal another glance at the TV screen, and catch a glimpse of a particularly odd episode, in which a deceased pool shark comes back from the dead to play one last game of pool against his living successor, it comes to mind, right now, my life is like a game of pool, a game of chance.

Like an episode of *The Twilight Zone*.

Like each day that I do something as simple as *waking up*, I *won* the game against the Big C once again.

Like my whole life right now, is nothing more

than a game of chance – or, in this case, a game of *faith*, my faith against the Big C – and, once again, I am the victor!

Sounds a little silly – or even a little morbid – I know, but, then again, if you were in my shoes? You might just feel the same way.

I hope you never have to, though.

#

To be honest?

Believe it or not, I am to the point now where I am actually looking *forward* to the chemo. I know that may sound sort of crazy to any one else who may be in my same position, but please, allow me to explain.

A human being can only take so much, whether it be either mentally or physically, before they reach the point of no return.

I am at that point *now*.

I wake up every day, sitting at my computer and typing up what may very well be my *last* story, yet, I feel no *fear* right now of what may come for me after I cross the threshold between life and death – and maybe beyond.

That's something else I've realized lately, when I look into the mirror each morning; dead is *dead*, and there is *no* in-between.

Meaning, I will no longer fear what I cannot *change*, especially because of the fact that, regardless of the uncertainty of the situation, the possible pain and discomfort and sickness that may still eat away at me, at least I faced it like a man, a *real* man, who refused to look death in the face and give up.

Death.

The *permanent* solution to a possibly *curable* problem.

So...bring on the chemo, I'm ready.

Or, as ready as I'll ever be, anyway.

FOURTEEN

Five days until chemo.

As usual, I'm sitting at my computer, typing away, the pain meds having given me a temporary reprieve from the cancer eating away at me.

Long enough to tell you a little about my Dad.

I have also realized lately that I am quite a bit like my Father – in a *positive* way, that is.

Unfortunately, my Father and I had drifted apart over the years, and had never bothered to make amends until it was too late to do so.

My father exuded an air of almost overbearing authority, ran the house with an iron hand, and his idea of parental responsibility was siring me, feeding me, making sure I did my homework and my chores. He wasn't necessarily cruel to me, but he wasn't necessarily kind to me, either. I was just *there*.

What I didn't understand at the time was, was too young and naive to understand, was my Father really *did* love me, but didn't know how to *show* it.

He had grown up in a totally different time that me, a totally different type of generation in general, one of respect and morals and strictness.

I had mistaken his strictness for meaness, when all he was really trying to do was make me a *man*, one of respect and morals and values, which, I had to admit now, I don't see too much of these days.

Trying to make a *man*.

A *tough* guy.

A...*survivor.*

Because he *loved* me.

#

Now, while I sit at my computer, I realize that more than ever before, and wish so much I had made the first move to reconcile with him before it was too late.

Instead, I was *stubborn*, and my Father died in a cold, clammy hospital bed, in a coma like state, gasping for breath until God mercifully took him home, where he belonged.

Where all good Fathers deserve to be.

Where I hope to see him someday, when God decides to take me home, too.

But for now, it's time to prove to my Father – and to myself – I really am like him; good, kind, respectful and brave enough to weather this storm known as cancer, do it with dignity and pride in myself, and hopefully live long enough to make him proud.

I *hope*.

FIFTEEN

Four days until chemo.

It's an unseasonably warm day for November, with a high of seventy degrees, with a sunny blue sky and fluffy white clouds floating by.

A perfect day for writing – and reflecting.

Today, my mind wanders back to a time when I thought I knew who my true friends really were – but was rewarded for my trust with a rude awakening.

I'm not really a big fan of social media, but I will have to admit, at times, it can wake you up with a hard slap in your face.

For example; since my cancer diagnosis was made public on Facebook, I had hundreds of *sincere* comments from a lot of people who were either simply a Facebook "acquaintance" or, total strangers.

I've even had well wishes and prayers from men and women who are well known actors in the film industry, as well as popular musicians and singers.

Total strangers.

But, I have had rare and few sincere posts or comments from people I have known since I was in gradeschool.

That's really hurtful at a time like this, you know?

But I intend to look at it this way; if this is how

much my *true* friends really care about keeping up with me and wishing me well, at least I know now not to waste any more valuable time dwelling on something that never really existed in the first place.

Oh, and by the way; any of my "true" friends need not bother showing up at my funeral, either. If you wouldn't even cross the street to wish me well when I was still alive, I don't need your drama after I'm dead and gone.

Just saying.

#

Otherwise, I'm having a pretty good day for a change, considering my current circumstances.

As usual, I'm in pain and feeling somewhat fatigued, but I am trying to make the best of it and spend a sunny day focusing on more positive things.

I'm getting out of the house for a change, heading to Walmart to do a little shopping, and pick up some much needed prescriptions at the pharmacy. After that, I'm headed to a nice burger joint here in town, to grab me a nice, big, juicy, greasy cheeseburger to enjoy before I have to begin my so called, "cancer diet" which I am sure will be just a tad bit more *bland* than the food I'm used to eating.

But...I'm not sitting here *smoking*, which is a good thing, right?

I just exchanged one vice for another one.

Okay...I'm a bad boy. Ha-ha.

But I think God will forgive me under the

circumstances.

#

Sitting at my computer again – as you can see.

I feel very lucky to have my computer. It's an off brand, almost ten years old, but, just like me, it's an old dinosaur that's still hanging in there, for better or for worse.

I've written a lot of good stories on this old computer, and some good books, too. I've actually made a little extra pocket money when I needed it, too, selling my stories and books on Amazon Kindle. I'm no Stephen King, but I don't do too bad, considering I'm just an unknown writer from a small town in Indiana.

I'm what you would call a "multi-genre" writer, too. I've dabbled in horror, science fiction, fantasy, and even true crime and local Indiana history. I've writtten coming of age stories, love stories, and I've even popped out a decent poem now and then.

Yep, my computer and I have entertained a lot of people out there. I've even sold books in England, France, Japan, China, Australia, and Italy.

People that live thousands of miles away, on the other side of the world have read my books.

Needless to say, I'm darn proud of that part of my life, anyway. No regrets.

I'm darn proud of ths book, too, the one you are reading now – although it may be my last.

I guess we'll see, won't we?

SIXTEEN

Three days until chemo.

I've been sitting here thinking about my upcoming appointment, the procedure in which I will receive my chemo port implant.

The thought of having some weird looking little gadget implanted into their chest might frighten some folks, and to be honest, I am a little nervous about it, but, considering the possible alternative, I'm going to suck it up and go along with the program.

I'm actually very lucky, to have had this happen at a time when our technology is so much far advanced than it used to be. A long time ago, if you were diagnosed with cancer – especially an *advanced* form of cancer – all a doctor could really do for you was give you something for the pain, make you as comfortable as possible, and then...well, wait for the end to come.

Nowdays, though, with so many different types of treatment to combat cancer, your chances of survival are much better, especially if it is diagnosed in the early stages.

So I shouldn't be worried, right?

You'd think not, but, as of recently, I am at *stage 3* in my cancer.

There are only *4 stages*.

#

So, I sit here and write my story.

While hoping I don't reach stage four.

But, if so, so be it.

I have a lot of people rooting for me; my brother, my kitty cat, what few real friends I have left, and, of course, my Heavenly guardians, my Mom, Dad, God, and Jesus Christ.

So, I think I have some darn good backup, don't you? I'd day so.

#

And, let's not forget my doctors – and one of my guardian angels, my oncology advocate, Kerri Pruitt.

Yes, I'd say I have all of my bases covered for now.

So, I write my story.

SEVENTEEN

Three days until chemo.

Sitting here at my trusty old Acer laptop, it feels more like I have three *weeks* until chemo. You know, time seems to *drag* along when you have something very unpleasant to deal with. It never fails.

But, that's okay. I have plenty of things to keep my mind occupied for now, like why my own son hasn't been by to see me, and wish me well.

Well, I know *one* reason he hasn't been by. He is still feeling too guilty to show his face.

Quite a few years back, my son had a bad problem with drugs, and, like most addicts with a monkey on their back, will do just about *anything* to get their next fix.

In my son's case, it was stealing money from his grandmother's purse. *My Mother's* purse.

That's when we lost all contact with him for quite a while, he was too ashamed to show his face for years afterward.

\#

As a matter of fact, it was eight years, to be exact, and by telephone, not in person.

He didn't even have enough respect or guts to apologize to my Mother face to face.

Or to me, either.

Long story short, since then – even after he found out I had cancer – he still hasn't dropped by to wish me well, or say he was sorry.

I look at it this way; it's very hurtful, yes. Do I wish things could have been different between us? Sure.

But, am I going to spend even a nano-second of what time I have left on this Earth dwelling on it? No sir, not me.

My son is a grown man, forty-five years old, and will have to spend what's left of his life, for all eternity, looking back on what he's done, and having to live with that guilt forever – and beyond.

Don't get me wrong; I love my son, and don't wish him any ill will, but, I do think his punishment fits the crime, so to speak.

I wish him the best; he's going to need it.

#

It's really funny – will, ironic, that is – how a man in my current position can sit back and think about such unpleasant subjects when he has cancer running through his veins.

I guess it comes with the territory, but, you'd think I would want to think about blue skies and birdies singing and eating a takeout pizza later, but instead, I have been thinking about something that most folks would want to forget.

But, since I've begun my journey with the Big C, I've noticed that God, in all of his infinite wisdom, has made sure that I have plenty of room in my memory palace for the things and people that have always been part of my life, and always will be, whether it be bad or good.

Plenty of room for forgiveness.

Plenty of room for redemption.

Plenty of room for *love*.

God is merely guiding me through the rough spots, so I'll be a better man when I come out on the other side.

When I *beat* the Big C.

So...until then, I will write my story, and be ever so thankful that God has graced me with yet another day on Earth to do so.

Amen.

Part 3
My Journey Begins

EIGHTEEN

Sunday, November 19th, 2023

Here I am again, sitting at my desk, typing away.

But today is somewhat different.

Somewhat, as I say.

Today is a day of very conflicting emotions. On one hand, I look forward to chemo, because it may just save my life. On the other hand, I dread it, because I know that chemo isn't going to be a day at the beach.

So many emotions, and only twenty-six hours to figure them out, or I'll be going in blind, so to speak.

Just sit here and think it all out, David, that little voice in my head tells me. *You can do it.*

But this time, the voice sounds like a whole cacophony of voices. No...a *symphony* of different voices; my Mother, my Father, and a lot of other loved ones who have passed before me, and then, in the middle of it all, the voice of *God*.

You can do this, David. You can do this, my child. My faithful one. My son.

Then I hear the joyous, playful sounds of my beloved pets that have passed before me; Bear the dog and Toby the cat and all the others, barks and meows all mixing together in an otherwordly symphony of joyous and playful laughter, a *Heavenly* sound. Of animal origin, yet Earthly, so sweet and soulful and comforting, just like they used to comfort me so long ago when I would be feeling so all alone.

So many wonderful voices, loud and boisterous yet calm and soothing, rooting for me.

Loving me.

Having faith in me.

So, I do what I always do at a time like this; I sit down at my trusty old Acer laptop and *write*.

It's the closest I can get to Heaven right now.

#

Last night, I had a vidid dream, that my Mother was here with me.

Not in human form, of course. Or Heavenly form, for that matter. She was just *there*, if that makes any sense. Her *presence* was there, I guess you could say.

In my dream, I was lying in bed, feeling very poorly, and all of a sudden I felt something, a gentle touch, like a hug, the kind of sweet hugs my Mother gave me as a child, so warm and soothing.

Then I heard her voice speaking to me, and although I couldn't make out what she said, I knew that knowing my Mother, it was something sweet and comforting.

Then I woke up.

A few minutes later, as I closed my eyes again, it didn't take me long at all to go back to sleep, and when I did, it was a peaceful one.

55

Was I just imagining things?
I don't think so.

#

That's yet another thing I've noticed about being within such close proximity with death.

I can hear and feel and even *see* so many wonderous things that I couldn't before the Big C took residence inside of me.

Oh, believe me, most of these wonderous things were already there, before the Big C came calling, but my eyes weren't quite open enough at the time for me to fully appreciate their meaning.

But I do now, and that's all that matters.

So...I write.

I will write good things and sweet things and loving things, stories that have a *positive* meaning, stories that will make others feel what I am feeling right now; *reborn*.

If this really is part of my rebirth, to suffer the Big C in order to come full circle within my own heart, then so be it.

I'm ready.

NINETEEN

November 20th, 2023 – 7 am
Four hours until chemo port surgery

Countdown has begun.

Sitting here at my trusty old Acer laptop, typing away, finding something to do besides think about the chemo.

I'm hungry and thirsty, but can't eat or drink because of the upcoming surgery. Can't even dry swallow a pain pill.

Oh yes...this is going to be an interesting day.

#

Well, maybe not an *interesting* day, but a *challenging* day, that's for sure.

They said I'd be in there at least seven hours; first, prep for the surgery. Then the surgery. They are going to place a sort of "implant" in my right upper chest, that will serve as a "port" to infuse me with the chemo drugs, as well as other different infusions, and for extracting blood for my lab work in the future.

A *permanent* implant, if it need be.

That sounds fun, doesn't it?

Okay, not really, but hey, I'm trying to keep my sense of humor intact under the circumstances, you know?

That's something else I learned about my current situation, is try to *always* keep a sense of humor about yourself, no matter how bad your day might seem to you at the time.

To be honest, I have smiled and laughed more lately than I had *before* I found out I had cancer.

But today, not so much. I guess I better find something to laugh about *before* I go to the hospital, huh?

Hmm...well, I can't seem to come up with much right now. Maybe later.

#

Well, as much as I hate to sign off for now, I must get ready to leave for the first part of my journey.

At least I get to take a shower before I go, make myself "presentable" before the main event. *A guy has to look and smell good before he gets poked and prodded and sliced up and infused! Ha-ha!*

See? There is that sense of humor I was talking about. *You have to keep your sense of humor.*

With that in mind, I will bid you farewell for now, and wish me luck!

But most of all, say a *prayer* for me, because I know God is watching over me.

TWENTY

November 21st, 2023 / 9 am

Well, here I am, still alive and kicking.

Surprisingly, I don't feel that bad.

Yet, that is.

But this feeling of uncertainty comes with the territory, so I just go with the flow.

I feel *very* lucky, just to be able to be sitting here at my computer, sharing my journey with you.

But I didn't feel so lucky yesterday, ha-ha.

#

From the time I walked in the door of the Cancer Pavillion, I could barely take another breath before I was being poked with needles { I could have sworn that lady drawing my blood was a vampire} taking my blood, taking this and that, stripping down and donning an open gown that as open in the back {hope the ladies enjoyed a peek at my skinny little booty!} and then wheeled out of my room toward other exciting adventures.

Like...surgery!

My chemo port!

Sounds like fun, doesn't it?
Believe it or not, it wasn't that bad.

#

Knowing what was coming my way that day, the general info having been conveyed to me by my guardian angel in residence, Miss Kerri Pruitt, I was going to make the best of it, and asked for a local anesthetic, so I could be awake during the surgery.

Purpose being, so I could make the general atmosphere – both mine and theirs – more enjoyable.

I'd made the right choice in doing so.

As soon as I was wheeled into the room, all of the ladies in there were joking around with me, playing music on the radio, and doing their best to make me feel comfortbable during this process.

Thank you ladies.

So I, in return, did my best to make them feel comfortable as well; I joked around with them, told them a funny little story, and told them about me being a writer, which they found to be pretty cool and interesting.

So...before knew it, the surgery was over, and I was wheeled back to my room to relax for a while before the main event...the dreaded chemo monster!

#

Yes...the dreaded chemo monster.

The monster whom I'd been dreading and dreaming about and worried about for so long. The monster whom, at this very moment, was coarsing through my veins like a runaway freight train, determined to get the best of me.

But what that little monster didn't know was, it had chosen the *wrong* guy to pick on.

Because I am a *tough guy*.

And I have *God* on my side.

I also have Kerri and all of the other great doctors and nurses and my chemo port all fighting for me, too.

How could I go wrong?

Amen.

TWENTY ONE

November 22st, 2023 / 8:30 am

Well, so far, so good.

No vomiting or diarrhea or extreme nausea.

My body feels pretty weak, though, like the chemo is draining all the nutrients and everything else that may be beneficial for good health from my body.

I Googled the Big C and the all mighty internet informed me that yes, cancer does tend to drain you in the way that it leaves your immume system pretty much open to attack – hence the Keytruda, an immunotherapy drug I reecived before the chemo – to help combat this feeling even more, and to guard your immune system.

But, it can be a real bummer too, when you feel drained already.

And so it goes.

So, I keep writing.

#

Iv'e noticed something about my writing recently I hadn't noticed before, too.

I tend to vent my frustrations in a more positive and harmless way, if nothing else. What we believe, why we believe –from nihilistic to religious–are a part of us and thus a part of our writing. We all have stories, mine is no better than anyone else's, all of us leading broken lives to one degree or another in this drama of life. And I find inspiration writing about redemption, about wringing hope from hopelessness.

I find solace in writing stories about those living on the fringe of society, yet not quite ever teetering over the edge of oblivion. I've been there, done that, so I'm most definitely writing what I know.

Some of these stories have a happy ending, some don't.

I am hoping – and of course praying – that the rest of my own story, whether it be a short or a longer version, will still serve a good purpose in the end.

I'd like to leave something positive behind after going through all of this, you know?

At this point in time, I think I will, but I'm still keeping my fingers crossed.

#

Of course, in the long run, luck has absolutely nothing to do with my recovery.

Sure, we all like to cross our fingers {or even your toes, if your feet are that limber} perform a coin toss for heads or tails, cut a deck of cards, for good luck, but it merely serves to *pacify* us – and only for a *short* period of time, too.

In the end? It is our faith and determination and our own, stubborn tenacity that may prevail in the end.

Which are all things I happen to possess – for

now, anyway – so that's one comfort in *my* favor, and believe me, I can use all the comfort I can get right now.

Also in my favor, I have my brother to help me through it all. He is five years older than me, has problems of his own, and still drives a school bus for extra income, but I swear, all I'd have to do in an emergency is snap my fingers and he would be right there, ready to help me.

Then there is my Mom and Dad, whom I am sure are watching over me from Heaven, and last, but not least, my favorite kitty cat, Holly Jean, who keeps me entertained and shows me unconditonal love and affection when I need it the most.

So...do I need luck?

Not really; I already have everything I need to battle the Big C.

TWENTY TWO

November 23rd, 2023 / Thanksgiving morning.

Thanksgiving day at the Boyer house...and my battle with the Big C rages on.

I was actually looking forward to the holiday, that is, until I *woke up*. Ha-ha.

All kidding aside, though, I had absolutely no idea I'd wake up feeling like *this*.

My onocology advocate, Kerri, had forewarned me of certain side effects, and unfortunately, I am one of the poor fellas who is going to have quite a few.

So far, I haven't used the bathroom {except to luckily be able to urinate} in seventy-two hours. All I do is cramp, my lower abdomen bloated like a balloon, and feel sick at my stomach.

Dizziness set in this morning, along with a terrible headache, and I have to walk outside, in the cold air, every twenty or thirty minutes, just to escape the feverish feeling that has taken over the upper half of my body.

Now, to make matters even worse, I am beginning to feel like a prisoner in my own home.

#

The longer I have to wear this chemo pack, and have to suffer the side effects, the more I feel like I am a *prisoner* to this cancer, and that makes me like it has *won*, it has *beaten* me already, and that *angers* me more than the side effects and discomfort ever will.

Yes, I realize by now all of this misery may just come with the territory, the natural order of things with chemo, but that fact doesn't make it any easier to deal with right now, and, unfortunately, *now* is where I am.

So...as usual, I do what I always do lately, to stifle the little cancer demons in my head and in my body – I sit down at my PC and write some more.

#

The terrible secret of my writing is that I don't have the imagination I used to have.

I recently published my last collection of short fiction – which, I must say, although it wasn't my best work by any means, wasn't my worst, either – still wasn't quite up to par. Point being, this cancer hasn't only robbed me of any sense of normalcy for now, it has also stolen, even if it is only briefly, of my once very over active imagination, and has replaced it with, yes, a whole big dose of *REALITY.*

There's an old saying that goes, "Truth is stranger than fiction," and I most certainly believe it now. Cancer, too, is one hell of a lot more *real* than fiction, that's for sure.

But, believe it or not, here I find inspiration again.

I guess you don't have to be a great writer,

though, to 'write what you know,' so here I am again, sitting here, writing what I know is the truth; I'm in for the biggest battle of my life, and I am no longer frightened than I am angry and vengeful against my new opponent, the Big C.

And I'm actually enjoying the fight now.

Come and get me, you son of a bitch! I say, to the Bic C. *You are not dealing with a weak man any longer, now you are dealing with ME.*

The NEW me.

To think, as I sit here drumming my fingers along this table waiting for inspiration to hit me, it was here already, all along.

I write because I feel I need to, to still the voices in my head. Because something in the core of my being crawls up and takes hold of me and says, YOU CAN DO THIS.

So...I continue to write, and, most of all, to fight.

It's all I have left, you know?

But it's enough for me.

TWENTY THREE

November 24th, 2023
Chemo pack removal day.

But, as usual, something else pops up to ruin my mood before I can even enjoy it.

Comes with the *territory*.

Lord, if I hear anyone who works within the medical field say that one more time, I think I'll puke.

Like I already haven't, that is.

Surely if something *comes* with the territory, it *goes* with it too, right? Well, I'm ready for it to *GO*.

#

Over the last few days, on the chemo, it seems as though instead of the side effects hitting me all at once, it's come in "phases."

For example, the first day, the side effects were exhausting.

Second day, *almost* tolerable.

Third day, not to much.

Fourth day, terrible; sore swollen, throat and tongue, nausea, extreme constipation, headache, dizziness, fatigue, and sleep deprivation. The pallor of my skin is ghost-like, and my eyes are bleary and bloodshot.

Yeah...I think I need a break.

#

I hadn't realized until recently, that this chemo drug coarsing through my veins is actually *poison*.

Sounds sort of crazy, right?

Like...*real* crazy?

Well, crazy it may be, but it's true.

Now, the chemo poison is a *good* poison {depending on you'd look at it, and as crazy as that may sound, too} and it is designed to gobble up all of those nasty little cancer cells and flush them out of your system.

But, there's a catch to this; you must be able to do the following things in order to help the poison stay on it's current course:

Maintain a decent, healthy diet, plenty of water to stay hydrated, be able to potty {both number one and two} on a regular schedule, get plenty of both sleep and exercise, but, at the same time, be able to perform all of the aforementioned duties while taking enough narcotic pain relievers, anti-nausea meds, and all of the other pills you would normally take, such as vitamin supplements, etc., at the *same time*. and still feel *almost* human.

All I can say is – and saying this from experience now – good luck.

#

But, as usual, I know this whole, seemingly relentless, overwhelming, and endless process has absolutely nothing to do at all with *luck*.

By some chance you feel "lucky" any time soon, and of course, not having to have suffered from the Big C in order to do so, think about this while you're basking in the glory of your so called "lucky streak." Next time you are feeling lucky, go on line and look up the definition of luck, and here's what you will find:

Chance considered as a force that causes good or bad things to happen.

Pay close attention to that first word; *chance.*

In other words, you'd have just as much "luck" cutting a deck of cards or flipping a coin or snapping your fingers, when it comes to dealing with chemo.

There is no luck involved with my current situation at all. Like I've said before {And I apologize for sounding like a broken record here} you must *fight.*

I mean, fight like you've never fought before, with all of your strength and determination you can muster to battle this foe that has invaded your body, or you will – and it might not be so *slowly but surely* this time – *lose* the battle.

Always remember; it doesn't make you weak to finally admit you are feeling defeated, and turn this whole mess over to God and Jesus Christ, and let them handle it.

Just saying.

TWENTY FOUR

November 25th, 2023
First day off of chemo pack.

I don't know if there is such a thing as chemotherapy wihtdrawls, but if there is, I'm going through them right now.

Upon waking up this morning, I was having almost violent like seizures, my whole body cold, clammy, and shaking. I took a well deserved, long, hot shower, and it seemed to help somewhat, but I'm still pretty shaky.

The shower was really nice, but my waterproof bandage came loose, but it didn't take me long to figure out why; when using a waterproof bandage, *shave* the area first, you dummy. Ha ha.

#

Sitting here at my computer now, typing away, sipping some nice cold Propel water to soothe my throat. It's working to a certain extent, but with each sip of that icy cold goodness also comes a good deal of pain, my tongue, the roof of my mouth, and my throat raw, sore, and swollen.

But at least I *can* swallow; yesterday, I could barely do so without losing my breath.

But, today is another day, I can swallow water, and next...let's see how I do with breakfast!

\#

Cream Of Wheat today, maple and brown sugar flavor, as a matter of fact.

Pretty tasty, too, other than the fact it tastes sort of like eating cardboard due to my taste buds being so numb.

Maple and brown sugar paper...yummy! - and yes, I was being sarcastic instead of optimistic.

So...sue me.

\#

Don't get me wrong; my pessimism doesn't necessarily stem from the fact that I am sick and suffering, more than it does the fact I know I am suffering because I did this to myself.

I am angry with myself.

Nobody else did this to me.

Not my ex-wife, nor my ex-girlfriend.

Not an good old friend who turned out not to be a good friend.

Not even fate or destiny or karma was involved in my downfall.

This was *my* fault.

Many years ago, my family practically *begged* me

to stop drinking and smoking – but as usual, to no avail.

My doctor – the same.

Did I listen?

Nope.

At the time, I was too self absorbed in self medicating myself each day just because my poor, pathetic excuse for a life wasn't kissing my selfish ass enough to make me happy at the time.

A breakup with a girlfriend? Hit that bottle.

Feeling nervous because of a hangover? Chain smoke those Marlboro menthol.

Feeling hungover and heartbroken both? Grab some of the hair of the dog that bit you – and chain smoke those cancer sticks.

I could always come up with a good excuse to slowly but surely self medicate myself into an early grave – and, needless to say, I almost did.

Until now.

Now, the *real* fight begins.

#

The real fight, for myself, didn't begin until I looked in the mirror, admitted it was *my* fault I had cancer, and then do something about it. Your own self awareness and admission about your cancer can help you too.

Speaking of which – and not to break away from the subject at hand for too long – but although I do understand now why so many people tried in vain to get me to straighten out my life, at the same time, I simply cannot stand listening to people berating and damning other folks over their past substance abuse issues.

Or any issue, for that matter.

Nobody, I mean absolutely NOBODY, is so high and mighty they have the right to damn other folks.

The person you are damning for their past actions are human, just like you.

They have families and wives and husbands and kids and friends just like you.

This person you whisper about as you pass by them in the grocery store? Their son or daughter may be in rehab for the fifth time – or worse yet, have died from a drug overdose.

Or...maybe they have just found out they are dying from cancer.

See where I'm going here?

This person doesn't need to be gossiped about or ridiculed or picked on. They need some *understanding*.

Sometimes, all they need some simple kindness, some compassion, forgiveness, and some support.

My brother and my doctors {and my kitty cat} showing me so much of these things is one of the only reasons I am sitting here writing this story.

Just saying.

TWENTY FIVE

November 25th, 2023 / early morning

Still sitting here, typing away...

Oh, yes, back to the subject at hand.

Your own self awareness and admission about your cancer can actually help you *heal*.

I'm not only referring to the physical aspect of your healing, either. There is also the *spiritual* healing that may be involved.

I'm no doctor – or philosopher – but I've been through enough physically to know that if you cleanse yourself mentally and spiritually first, then your physical healing may begin without any negative factors in the way to impede the process – and your progress.

Which is, in my shoes, much better than no progress at all.

But for now, my friends, I must bid you farewell so I may take a much needed break from my daily routine, so I may be bright eyed and bushy tailed to conitinue in the morning.

Night night, my friends, and sweet dreams.

I know I could use a sweet dream or two.

TWENTY SIX

November 26th, 2023, early morning

Well, I wasn't graced with any sweet dreams, but I was blessed with a good night's sleep for a change. No mattter, really; my sweet dreams normally turn into nightmares, anyway.

I did wake up with diarrhea.

Also included in my pre-breakfast journey into a real life hell on Earth was indigestion and coughing up bile from my throat. Yummy!

#

This might just sound a tad bit odd, but I think I felt *better* while I was on the chemo bag.

Seriously, folks.

At least when I was on the chemo bag. I felt sort of...well, numb, I guess you could say. But now that the chemo is absent from the daily routine, it seems like my whole body, from head to toe, has suddenly turned itself inside out, and is...well, is craving some type of nourishment. I'm not sure how to describe it exactly, that would make any common sense to someone who hasn't been through this before.

Best I can do for now is to say I wish it would

stop before I just break down and cry, beg for mercy.

#

There is one bright spot coming up soon.

My 64th birthday is coming up in about a week, and I fully intend to enjoy it to the fullest of my human ability, whether I feel like it or not. In my position, you don't want to waste any valuable time you have left {or may not have left} focusing on all of the negative aspects of the situation 24-7.

This year, on my birthday, my wish is not for any fancy birthday cake, expensive gifts, or even a birthday card. My birthday wish this year is for *one* thing, and one thing *only.*

To hear my doctor tell me that my cancer is going away.

To hear that one and only wonderful word all cancer patients long to hear.

Remission.

That would be the *best* gift of all.

#

Sitting here right now, typing away again, it suddenly came to me; writing isn't the only pastime I've enjoyed over the years.

I have always enjoyed reading, too.

Until I began helping my mother take care of my ailing father back in 2007, I was a voracious reader, and spent a lot of my spare time at our local library, sometimes renting up to five or six books at one time.

Stephen King was one of my favorite writers back then, and not only because he wrote a lot of horror fiction {as I did at the time, too, selling my short stories to on line magazines} but also because of his general outlook on life at the time.

Stephen King once stated that at times, we tend to "create our own horrors in order to deal with the real ones." I may be wrong, but I think what he meant that we all, at one time or another, tend to dream up our own little "creative outlet" so to speak, to deal with the bad things going on around us.

For him – and for me back then – it was writing and reading. So, since I could most definitely use my own little "outlet" to escape my sorry life right now, why not?

Point being, believe it or not, there is, more often than not, *something* you can do to get your mind off dealing with the after-effects of chemo, and it will be better than just sitting around feeling sorry for yourself.

Believe me, I *know*.

TWENTY SEVEN

November 27th, 2023, early morning

Bad day again today, *must keep busy.*

Sometimes, I even read my own books, and lately, I have realized, with eye opening clarity, that I am better at non fiction than I am at any other genre.

Not to say I can't still come up with a good fictional tale now and then; I was recently informed by one of my Facebook friends that one of my fictional stories really threw them for a loop with it's totally unforseen "twist ending."

But, overall, I'd say that my non-fiction books – like this one – tend to be a much better example of my capability as a writer. Not trying to toot my own horn here, just stating fact.

Well...maybe I was tooting my own horn just a little bit. Ha-ha.

#

Speaking of tooting my own horn, once upon a time, I even wrote a screenplay based on an original story by yours truly.

Really, I did.

It was a sweet little coming of age story entitled, "Mystery, Indiana,"{which was actually based on my life growing up in my hometown of Vincennes, Indiana}and it was about a young boy who meets a beautiful young girl at the local beach one day, falls in love at with her first sight, and then she suddenly disappears.

Yeah, I know, sounds so cliché, right? It's been a million times. Not so.

In my story, she disppeared – and of course reappeared – because she is a *ghost.*

I know...sounds sort of goofy, huh?

Well, it may *sound* goofy, but, *five* different indie filmmakers from Indiana wanted to produce it for a feature film – but, we didn't have the budget, which would have been around three-hundred-thousand dollars.

I know...by now you're thinking, so, what's your point? What does that have to do with your battle with cancer?

Point *being,* I am thinking about not only resubmitting the script to some local filmmakers, but I'm also thinking about writing a screenplay about my battle with cancer, sort of a *documentary* film. Even if the film was released *posthumously,* and I never got to watch it, maybe it would help somebody else deal and cope with their own battle with the Big C after I was gone.

I think it's a grand idea myself.

#

But for now, I must adjorn from my computer for the day, walk over to the hospital for some blood work {and hopefully some pain relief from the Army of nasty little cancer buggers that are currently having a party in my mouth and throat} and come back home and hopefully take a nap.

I hope so, anyway.

Then again, I am referring to a day in *my* life, right? So...we'll see, won't we? Ha-ha.

TWENTY EIGHT

November 28th, 2023, early morning

Well, things didn't quite turn out as I had hoped.

Imagine that.

Apparently, the nasty little bacterial buggers that set up shop in my mouth over the weekend have literally infested my entire mouth, throat, and even the mucous membranes of my nasal cavity.

Believe me, folks, if you look back on your youth, and recall how painful tonsillitis was, that is nothing compared to this.

As I've said before, I'm not pitching for a pity party, mind you, just stating plain fact, for the sake of those who may be reading this book. Any pity – if any at all – I might have felt for myself is long gone.

#

By now – by page 78 of my so called "magnum opus" - you may have considered me long winded, repetitive, or, God forbid, even boring – and, if so, I apologize.

But at the same time, if I have happened to make to make you feel this way, please excuse me if I don't offer any long winded apologies, either. One of the main reasons I wrote this book is to *help others*.

Now, onward we go...

\#

After consulting with my onocology advocate – and doing some on line research, of course, - I have a short but sweet list of inexpensive, homemade remedies for those of you who may not have affordable insurance and may be on a very tight budget to boot.

First of all, for the sore gums, and the roof of your mouth, you may try the following remedy:

One 6 ounce of warm water

One full teaspooon of salt

One full teaspoon of baking soda

Mix well in a glass, take a sip, swishing the mixture around in your mouth slowly for sixty seconds, making sure not to swallow any of the mixture, then spit it out, then rinsing your mouth with cool water.

This mixture is also good for gargling, which is also good for the sore throat.

Note, this is only for *temporary* relief; if the pain and discomfort persists, please contact your doctor ASAP for a professional to prescribe something for you.

Now, back to my day...

\#

Ah, yes, I was talking about my day.

So far, not so good.

But, as always, {as you can see} I log on to my trusty old Acer laptop, and carry on with my daily routine. Yeah, I know... *boring!!!*

But, at least I'm *alive* to do it, right?

As I sit here, typing away, I am once again reminded of a time in my past when I was suffering from a severe case of the dreaded writer's block, and how funny {not ha-ha funny, more like ironic} that now that I have cancer, it's like a magical doorway has suddenly appeared in my office, a doorway into a whole new dimension, a new *world*, where all I have to do is push a power button on my PC, and...*voila!*

No more writer's block!

But to be totally honest, I could have done without the cancer. Ha-ha.

Yes, I said "Ha-ha." Always remember; on those not-so-good days – or just a plain old completely rotten old day – find *something* to make you laugh or at least crack a big smile.

I don't care if it's watching your favorite TV sitcom or funny movie or reading a funny story or, better yet, call an old friend that could always make you laugh, and chat for awhile. Who knows? You might just make their day – and make them laugh or smile, too.

Just saying...

Well, I must bid you farewell again for now; my sore, hungry little belly is telling me it's high time for some of what I now refer to {not so fondly} as my "between chemo treatment" diet food. On today's lunch menu we have potato soup with Ritz crackers and a glass of milk.

Yummy!

Until we meet again...

TWENTY NINE

November 29th, 2023, early morning

Well, I woke up feeling a might peaked again, but I'm still hanging in there, thank the Lord.

No writer's block, either, which is a good thing, because this chapter is special to me, by far more than some of the others, not to say they didn't hold a special meaning too, of course.

On to the story.

As I sat here again this morning typing away, feeling as though my body was betraying me me again – which it actually is, of - my mind suddenly drifted back to the last time I saw my best friend from gradeschool, Philip, one day, as I stood outside in the yard watering the flowerbed.

It was beautiful Summer day, with a nice breeze and perfect for just about any type of outdoor activity. As I stood there, taking it all in, he happened to be driving by and stopped to chat for a few minutes, which for me was a welcome distraction from my daily routine.

I hadn't seen him for a while, and upon seeing him up close and personal, I could see that, although he seemed to *feel* bright eyed and bushy tailed, his body had continued to betray him over the years as well. A crippling back injury, I believe it was, and from there things didn't really improve much for him.

Sadly, he passed away last year from a heart attack, no doubt prompted by his health issues, and I still haven't gotten over his passing – don't imagine I ever will – and still think about that last day I saw him, his own body still betraying him, but Philip just shrugging it off as easily as he would swat an annoying fly.

That day, when seeing how his body had betrayed him as well, and how such a strong man, not only physically but also in heart and soul, was still capable of a warm smile, a firm handshake, or a big hug when someone would need it, yet ended up this way, it didn't seem quite fair.

Don't get me wrong, I learned a long time ago that life isn't always fair {especially at those times we are having a bad day} but I couldn't help but feel that way at the time.

He didn't allow his health problems to slow him down or keep him locked up 24-7 or lose his love for others or his sense of humor or anything else that made him who he was. He fought the good fight until the day the good Lord took him home.

He was not only a good friend to me, he was in *inspiration*.

So, I am going to try to be just like he was when he was battling his own health condition, and fight the good fight until the Lord calls me home too.

NEVER GIVE UP.

Don't worry, Philip. I won't give up.

THIRTY

November 30th, 2023, early morning

Something else I do not intent to give up on in the very near future is the idea of eating cake.

Birthday cake, that is.

I will be sixty-four-years old this Monday, and nothing, I mean *nothing*, is going to stop me from eating my cake. It could a swollen sore throat or a swollen tongue or canker sores or loose teeth or even the bubonic plague, I am *eating my cake*.

Don't get me wrong, I know there are a lot more important things to be concerned with right now, but, at the same time {and not to sound purposely morbid} if you are afraid you may *not* see your *next* birthday, simple food items like cake, cookies, and candy seem a lot more special to you then.

Just saying...

#

Sitting here day dreaming of cake, my mind wanders back to my youth, when my mother and I would spend Saturday mornings in the kitchen making all sorts of delicious cookies and cakes and pies with my grandmother Engle's old recipe book.

Homemade peanut butter cookies was my favorite.

Back in those days, it was all made from *scratch*, too. Flour, sugar, baking soda, baking powder, eggs, peanut butter, vanilla extract, all of it mixed up from scratch and baked up fresh in the oven.

One of the main things I remember about the days we were baking was the *smell* coming from the kitchen, too. Well, I wouldn't call it a smell, more than an *aroma* of stuff baking in the kitchen. There was absolutely nothing like the aroma of cookies baking in the kitchen, and the anticipation of getting to eat a cookie fresh out of the oven with a big glass of ice cold milk.

By the time we were done, the kitchen would be a big mess, but I was more than glad to help clean it up if it meant getting to nibble on those tasty cookies for the next few days.

Wow...how I miss those days now.

But, once again, these oh-so-sweet memories give me even more inspiration to keep moving forward with my book, and knowing my mother is up there watching over me, so proud of me, and so touched by my sweet memories of our days baking together.

So...yes, I will move forward once again, and make myself and my mom proud, and, most of all, I will beat the Big C at it's own evil game, once and for all, and be alive to sign copies of this book in person for all of my friends.

Amen.

THIRTY ONE

November 30th, 2023, late morning

Yep, still sitting here, eating some lukewarm cream of wheat and typing away at my trusty old Acer laptop.

Not sure what's going to be on the lunch menu just yet, but I hope it will be something I can swallow without being in a lot of pain.

For some odd reason my onocology doctors haven't quite figured out yet, the pills they gave me to ease the discomfort in my mouth and throat – as well as KILL the bacteria that's causing it – is not working. I can do something as simple as swallow lukewarm water and it goes down like broken glass.

But, as always, I'm hanging in there.

It's all I *can* do.

#

So...here I am.

For better or worse.

For richer or poorer.

In sickness and in health.

Until death do me part.

I may now kick the Big C's ass.

Amen.

#

Hey, I have to keep a sense of humor about it all, you know? If not....well, I don't even want to *think* about that.

So...I type.

Click click click click click go the keys!

Ouch ouch ouch ouch ouch goes my throat!

Oh Lord, my stomach feels *SO* empty.

Oh dear Lord, PLEASE let me eat ANYTHING without pain! Just a donut. Or a piece of pumpkin pie. Or cake. A cookie? Sure! Bring it on. Something soft and creamy and yummy and special just for me, okay?

Oh man...I am DYING for a piece of chocolate.

But...as much as I hate to admit it, there is something else I'm dying for more than sweets or takeout burgers or pizza.

I'm dying for a drink.

An *alcoholic drink.*

#

Yes, I am on the verge of destroying almost *seventeen years* of sobriety.

That is, I *was* on the verge of doing so.

I've been down up and down this old lonely road known as alcoholism so many times – twenty-five years on the bottle, seventeen years off now – that I'm definitely no stranger to the temptations of what I refer to as the *demon* alcohol.

I close my eyes, and it almost seems like it was yesterday...

...I'm sitting in a rear corner booth in Bud's tavern, a known haunt for the walking wounded when they are looking for love in all the wrong places Under the crimson glare of the bar's lights, I stare out at a sea of empty lives.

Men and women searching for the momentary distraction of drunken comradery to numb themselves from the pain of their own reality. The décor reeks of a pervasive hopelessness that has settled even into the Formica tables; an air of desperation as thick as the spent Scotch fumes from the nearby table...

But, once again, I am doing my best to control my old urges, stay on the straight and narrow path to success, and resist taking a leisurely stroll down to the package liquor store.

It is here, once again, I find more valuable inspiration.

#

It may sound odd to someone who has never suffered with a substance abuse problem, but at times, a person who has been "around the block" a time or two, is the type of person who can give you the best advice on how to conquer your *own* addictions.

Not to sound self righteous, mind you, or sound as though my past experiences with alcoholism make me some sort of genius. I'm just making my point all too clear that no matter how hopeless things may seem to you right now – the cancer, the chemo or radiation, the pain, the worry...yes, it can all be so damned frightening and overwhelming.

But absolutely no amount of alcohol, addictive drugs, or anything else you can dig up to self medicate yourself will help you. At best, it will only serve to provide you with a *temporary* solution to a *permanent* problem.

You are trying to *heal*, not suffer even more.

Just saying.

THIRTY TWO

December 3rd, 2023, late morning.

It seems like the first two days of the new month have gone by like a blur.

I woke up today with yet another affliction – like I really needed another one.

But at least this one is curable, if I really set my mind to it.

I feel like I'm beginning to do something I thought I'd never do; lose my sense of humor.

For most of my life, up until now, I have always managed to find at least one thing humorous about my day. Whether it be a funny TV show or a joke someone tells me or, as the age of the internet kicked in, a funny meme or amusing Facebook post from a friend.

But today?

Nothing.

Not one thing can make me laugh. I can't even work up a giggle, let alone a smile.

To make matters worse, I feel like a hypocrite, after spouting off all of this great advice on how to make yourself feel better.

Yet, here I am, unable of even cracking a grin or even *forcing* a smile.

This has been the worst day yet, and it's *not* getting better this time.

#

My life is definitely interesting right now. I wake up early every day glad to be alive, spend most of the day trying to find reasons why it's great to be alive, then can't wait to go to bed at night to *escape* my life.

Weird feeling.

This demon known as cancer is really messing with my heart and soul. Never let's me get myself together long enough to enjoy one day without reminding me it's still there, torturing me just a little bit more than before.

Like it's actually an evil thing that enjoys what it's doing to me.

I wish I could have ONE day that's NORMAL again.

But so far, on this day, the day before my 64th birthday, all I see on my horizon is pain, misery, and yes, finally, hopelessness.

Happy Birthday to me.

THIRTY THREE

December 4th, 2023, early morning.

My so called, "birthday."

If only I could *EAT* something.

My tongue feels like it's coated with acid. Some type of "bacterial bile" forms on the surface of my tongue at night while I sleep, and I wake up off and on all night, having to wipe it off with sterile pads, and spit the rest out in a cup.

Happy Birthday!

I talked to my so called "on call" doctor, yesterday, and she informed me that apparently some blood test and possibly some antibiotics may be in order for my current dilemma.

I hope so. It would be nice to choke down a piece of my strawberry pudding cake past my sausage size tongue without any pain. Just saying.

Yes...I am feeling pretty pitiful today.

#

I'm not exactly pity party material yet, but I'm getting there fast.

I know, I know; *don't give up now, David! You've come too far to let the Big C get you down! It's your birthday! Don't allow it to beat you down today!*

There goes that little voice in my head again. The voice of understanding, of reasoning, when I need it the most. That voice I used to recognize so well, my *own* voice.

It speaks to me now, on my 64th birthday, trying it's level best to let me know I'm really not *alone* in this; there are plenty of folks out there rooting for you, wishing you well, wishing you a Happy Birthday.

Praying for you.

Making you feel loved and appreciated when you really need it the most.

As I now stop typing away long enough to check out my Facebook page, I see that so many of my Facebook friends and acquaintances have already wished me a happy birthday:

Happy Birthday, David! Have a blessed day!

Prayers for your healing and comfort!

Happy Birthday, old friend! You've got this, don't let it beat you down!

Happy birthday David! Have the best day possible!

Continued prayers for you!

Well, you get the idea.

I know I do.

Once again, when all seemed so hopeless and painful and sad, there it was, the whole time.

One of – if not the *best* reasons – to be happy and thankful for all that I have, and, in addition to all of this love and support, maybe my doctors will find a way to end this pain today, at least temporarily.

I am a very simple man, it doesn't take all that much to make me happy. If I could just eat a decent meal, and some cake, without any pain, for just a *few minutes*, I'd be happy.

So, maybe, just maybe, I could have a really good birthday in the end. After all, look at all I really *do* have to be thankful for.

Well, my wall clock is telling me it's time to head over to the hospital now.

I would say, "wish me luck," but I've already received all that I need in the way of prayer.

THIRTY FOUR

December 5th, 2023, early morning.

Well, my 64th birthday wasn't completely uneventful after all.

Once again, as I do from time to time, I received both good news – and bad news.

I'll just get the bad news out of the way first, tear the old band aid off quick, so to speak. Bad news is, the pain in my mouth is here to stay for now.

I had received such a strong, aggressive chemotherapy treatment the first time, it has left certain areas of my body weak and open to these types of problems.

All I can do for now is take my pain meds, use the Magic Wash and Mugard for the mouth and tongue pain, and hope it tapers off before my next chemo treatment next week.

I have also lost a total of twenty-three pounds in the last few weeks, which has made me feel weak too. I need to eat more healthy food in the future too, gain weight back. But she did say that I could eat all of the ice cream and pudding I want!

I absolutely must have my so called, "creature comforts."

\#

Speaking of which, as I sit here at my trusty old Acer laptop, typing away again I am jamming to some of my favorite bands from the 60s and 70s.

First, a little Pink Floyd {and some of my pain meds} to make me feel, "Comfortably Numb," then, as I settle in for a marathon writing session, a little of The Rolling Stones, to make me feel like a "Beast of Burden."

But today, unlike a lot of other days, I feel no real burden except for the one of pain, whom, unfortunately, is my constant companion, yet at the same time, reminds me I'm still alive and kicking, which as always is much better than the alternative.

So...I sit back, close my eyes, take a deep breath, exhale, then repeat the process several more times.

Now I'm in the *ZONE*.

My zone.

The zone in which, no matter what may be going on around me – or to me – I am the Master of my domain, the King of my castle, and the Prince of my own *fate* – at least for *now*.

My zone is a *good* place today.

So...I *type.*

THIRTY FIVE

December 6th, 2023, early morning.

I don't feel too bad today, considering how my day ended yesterday.

For some reason, by late afternoon, I ended up with a terrible case of upset stomach and diarrhea that didn't quite taper off until almost bedtime.

I know by now that this is nothing new when it comes to the so called "after effects" of a massive dose of chemo, but it doesn't help to serve the purpose of consuming – and maintaining – a healthy diet.

Calories aren't calories if your body doesn't even have a chance to absorb them.

So...yesterday morning? Not bad. Last night? Not so good. Comes with the territory; a couple of bottles of Propel water and some anti- diarrhea medicine and I'll be as good as new.

#

But for now, I'm typing away again, counting my blessings, and feel lucky to be alive for another day.

Today is a special day, too; you know why?

Because I *want* it to be a special day.

Yep, it's that simple.

You know *why* it's that simple?

That's the easy part.

Just in case you have forgotten already, I am the Master of my domain, the King of my castle, and the Prince of my own *fate* – at least for *now*.

So...if I *say* it is a special day, it *IS* a special day for me.

Today, on my "special day" I intend to spend it not only working on my new book {as you can see} but I am also going to watch a true crime documentary on Netflix {I have "dabbled" in the true crime genre myself on several ocassions, and with some relative success} eat a big, heaping bowl of French vanilla ice cream, and chill out like the lazy old fart that I am, and enjoy every second of it.

By some chance my ice cream immediately performs an about-face, and comes screaming back out like a big white rocket from the planet UR-Anus, then so be it. I'll just pop some more anti-pooping pills, and go back to spoiling myself.

I can be a very, *very* stubborn man where it concerns my creature comforts.

So...onward I go!

THIRTY SIX

December 7th, 2023, early morning.

I'm still a little dehydrated from yesterday, but otherwise woke up pretty much unscathed.

So far, that is.

But I'm keeping up the faith!

#

I started a new pain med prescription today, a higher dosage, which I'm told will help with the pain in my mouth and tongue, which should make it easier for me to eat, which I'm hoping {and praying, of course} will work out.

I have plenty of snacks that are easy to eat – pudding, ice cream, and plenty of soups and hot cereal like oatmeal – so I should be okay for now. What I'm sort of dreading, though, is the fact that if I don't get my white blood cell count back up by Monday the 11th, and my mouth is still like this, I've been told I might not be placed back on my chemo treatments for another week, which of course means a *delay* in my treatments.

I never thought I'd see the day when I would dread *not* getting chemo, but I have. *Weird...*

Time to sign off for now.

THIRTY SEVEN

December 10th, 2023, early morning.

Oh, that's just great.

When I got out of the shower this morning, I noticed my hair was thinning out, and I doubt it's from my age, either.

I knew that chemo could cause hair loss, but I was hoping it wouldn't happen this soon. I guess I'll order me some "do-rags" from Amazon, and at least try to be fashionable about it. Ha-ha. I can see it now; folks will be calling me Snoop Dog at the chemo center.

Oh well. I am sixty four years old now, so at least some partial baldness or a receding hairline isn't all that uncommon.

I just wasn't *ready* for it.

Then again, when has the Big C ever cut me a break yet? Sneaky little devil, it is. Always lurking in the shadows, ready to pounce on me whenever I'm actually having a decent day.

Oh well. I guess I'll be saving money on hair gel this month, huh?

#

Yep, tomorrow morning, it's time for my second round of chemo. I *think*.

Not sure yet. Damn white blood cell problem and all. One thing for sure about the Big C; it's always predictable – and unpredictable – on a regular basis.

If not, I'll just try to make the best of the day, as usual, and move on. If so, then I'll still try to make the best of the day, and have my little chemo bag buddy to haul around with me, hopefully making me better, opening a can of whup-ass on the Big C.

I hope.

Hope and faith is all I have at times, you know? Then again, at times, hope and faith are all I need.

#

But for today, I'll just concentrate on something at least a bit more positive.

Ice cream and Netflix? Why not?!

A big, juicy, crème filled donut? Oh yeah!

A pizza?! Cheese and sausage from Bobe's Pizza house, please!

Hey, a guy has to enjoy life now and then, right? Besides, I need to gain a few pounds back, right?

Good enough reason for me.

So...until tomorrow...

THIRTY EIGHT

December 11th, 2023, early morning.

Sitting here, watching that clock...

Chemo day.

Maybe.

It will all depend on how I feel, what my white blood cell count may be, and other factors involved, such as my ability to eat without pain, etc.

Should be an interesting day, to say the least.

I guess we'll see, won't we?

#

Well, that was a short visit.

No chemo today. I was told my white cell blood count was still a bit off, and my mouth needed to heal a bit more before another round of chemo. As it is, the doctors are going to cut the strength of my infusion down thirty percent, in order to avoid so many bad side effects in the future.

So, for now, a short and sweet vacation is in order, and I'm ready!

THIRTY NINE

December 13th, 2023, early morning.

Today is social security day! Yippee!

Time for shopping and paying bills and then kicking back and chilling out. I know, I know; sounds kinda boring, huh? But to a guy in my position, it's not only a happy day to look forward to, but a Godsend as well.

I feel very lucky to receive my SS payments. Just like I feel lucky to still be *alive* to enjoy them. It's really odd how, at one time, I dreaded getting older and taking retirement and chilling out in my recliner. Then the Big C decided to sneak up on me, and...BOOM!

I felt lucky to even wake up and have a normal bowel movement. Ha-ha.

So, yes, my SS day is very important to me. It reminds me of how much older I am, sure, but it also reminds me of how lucky I am to be here and spend it.

So...onward to the Dollar General Store for some grocery shopping!

#

Something else I actually enjoy about being retirement age; shopping.

I used to hate grocery day. It was my own impatience, I guess, not wanting to concentrate all that much on food of any nutritional value, and instead grabbing a lot of cheap, easy to fix foods such as Ramen noodles and TV dinners and soda pop and sweets.

Not so now days; I walk through the aisles, slowly, taking my time, picking out more healthy choices, knowing that the food I'll be consuming now will help me live longer in the end. Don't get me wrong; I still munch on the ocassional donut or candy bar, and I love my nightly bowl of ice cream while I watch TV, but otherwise? It's my health first, and my creature comforts come in second.

At times, as odd as it may sound, I feel as though my cancer might end up *saving* my life.

Stranger things have happened, believe me.

Like...divine intervention, perhaps?

We'll see.

FORTY

December 14th, 2023, early morning.

Well, I had a good shopping day.

I bought all sorts of healthy foods as well as a bunch of nice, fatty foods, to fatten up my skinny, cancer stricken ass.

It's a hard line to draw, actually; between good food and bad food. Especially when your onocologist is telling you to eat healthy one minute, and telling you to eat a bowl of ice cream topped with vanilla pudding the next minute.

I have to look at it this way; I get to enjoy the best of *both* worlds, right?

Always think *positive*.

Some days, it's all you have.

#

But today is a positive day, and I intend to do some positive things with my time.

As you can see, I'm working on the book again. Also on the agenda; a healthy lunch, followed by ice cream and Netflix. Sounds pretty good for a day in the life of a cancer patient, right? Well, sometimes it's okay, other times, not so much.

Some days, I would give almost *anything* to leave this house, my own little private prison, and take a long walk in the sunshine. Listen to the birdies singing in the trees, watch the squirrels run along the power lines and the neighborhood kittys cats gather at my door wanting snacks.

Just anything to feel *free*.

Feel free from these four walls.

Feel free from my TV chair.

Feel free from this cancer, and from my life in general.

But it's not to be.

So...I sit down at my trusty old Acer laptop and I *write*.

Sometimes, my writing sets me free, too.

#

But not today.

Today, I feel all alone here again, and wish I had something more to do than sit here and think about my cancer and my hair falling out, and my throat and tongue always sore when I eat.

I have my good days and my bad days.

Cancer is good for that, you know. Some days it wakes up and says, *Have a good day! Today you'll feel pretty decent, so you better not waste it!*

Then on other days, it says, *Oops, sorry! Today is really going to be a pain in the ass, and you're going to hate every last second of it! I do have a job to do, you know!*

Yes, believe me, I *know*.

So...I write some more.

I have a job to do, too, Mr Cancer. Mr constant pain in my ass. Mr Big C.

My job today, is to make sure you don't beat me down too much, so I can wake up again tomorrow morning, and write about my battle with you.

How I beat *you* down instead. Keep you at bay while I wage my battle against my sworn enemy. Yes, you heard me, Mr C.

I'm *still* here.

You better take your best shot, because I intend to be right back here tomorrow morning, too.

I'm ready.

FORTY ONE

December 15th, 2023, early morning.

Here I am, back again!

I feel a little droopy, but that's nothing new. Other than that, I don't feel too bad.

I woke up hungry, too, which is always a good sign. When the Big C has paid you a visit, and the after effects of the chemo are still lingering, and you are lucky {or blessed} enough to wake up hungry and thirsty, you should be grateful.

I am.

But, first things first.

I must write.

#

Yes, as I sit here today, eating some maple and brown sugar flavored cream of wheat, I can honestly say I feel very blessed today.

It's not every day I can say that, so I am definitely feeling good right now, very optimistic about what the day may hold for me. Whether it be good or bad, I fully intend to make the best of it. It's all I *can* do.

Oh, and I hope whoever may be reading this book has been enjoying it. I hope it has opened your eyes to just what, exactly, a cancer patient has to go through, in order to fully understand their current state of health and frame of mind, to not only make it easier for them, but yourself as well.

A cancer patient has only *one* specific goal, too, which is getting *better.* They want to hear that beautiful word, that one word that will make all of the hurt and fear and pain go away.

Remission.

Oh, what a *beautiful* word it is.

Another beautiful word is *hope*.

Because without hope, you have nothing to look forward to each day. Hope – and prayer – is the main foundation of your every day existence.

That and ice cream.

And pudding.

Hey, you *have* to include your creature comforts in there somewhere, you know?

With that thought in mind, I shall now bid you farewell until tomorrow, when I shall return to grace you with even more bits of wit and wisdom.

And, hopefully, more good news.

I *hope*.

FORTY TWO

December 16th, 2023, early morning.

Only two days until chemo again...and the countdown has begun!

Seriously, though, I'm kinda looking forward to it. A guy in my postion can only go so long before he as to admit to himself it's for the betterment of his health to go under the dreaded chemo needle again.

So many mixed emotions...tearing me apart from both sides...

Yet, here I am. Still fighting the good fight. Still hanging on by a thread, yet still hanging on.

It is the story of my life, and it is an interesting one to say the least.

#

On today's agenda, first, I write.

Then, who knows what interesting and exciting things I might find to occupy my time, and my mind. The possibilities are endless.

That's the problem on certain days; the possibilities are much *too* endless for my own good. I need something *fresh*, something *new*, to occupy my time. Don't get me wrong. I am very thankful for the things I do have, but, after so long, some of them seem *very boring*.

For example; my TV set. I have a very nice 40 inch flat screen TV with 150 channels and even Netflix. You'd think with that many channels to choose from, I'd never have to suffer from boredom.

Yet, I do.

You'd think that with tons of DVDs to watch and books to read – even my own books – I'd never be bored, yet, I am.

You'd think that with a sweet, loving little kitty cat running around the house, I'd never be lonely, yet I am.

Thus goes the story of my life with the Big C.

My constant companion, the Big C.

Always there to keep me company. When I'm lonely? There is the Big C, to wrap it's not-so-loving arms around me in a death embrace.

I guess I'm never *really* alone, am I?

This chapter is beginning to sound a bit morbid, isn't it?

Time to sign off for today, get my head together.

FORTY THREE

December 17th, 2023, early morning.

Countdown has *officially* begun; twenty-three hours and ten minutes until chemo.

My hair is still falling out.

Even my eyebrows are getting thinner.

Pretty soon, I will look like a either a sideshow attraction or a mannequin, one or the other. This should be fun.

Just one more damn thing to make me feel awkward or self consicous about my appearance.

Just what I *don't* need.

But that's my story for today.

#

And every other day lately.

As I stand in front of the bathroom mirror, combing yet another layer of hair from my scalp, it suddenly dawns upon me; maybe the ladies will think you look handsome this way. There are bald movie stars, you know?

Then I comb yet another layer of hair from my scalp, and think, no, because you aren't rich and famous.

You're a two-bit writer from a small town in Indiana who is currently experiencing dellusions of grandeur because he is feeling so goofy otherwise.

Can't wait for my mustache and beard to fall out, too. I'll look like a bowling ball with eyes.

Wait...that's the ticket!

Learn to make *fun* of yourself.

Learn to laugh along with anything life throws at you, and make a *joke* out of it. And, always remember; a friend, a *true* friend, isn't laughing *at* you, they are laughing *with* you.

That's the ticket!

So, I continue combing and laughing and then moving on with my day.

It's all I can do.

#

I may be smiling, but it's under protest.

But it's what I need to do, for the overall betterment of my day. SMILE.

Laugh, giggle.

Make fun of myself.

Well, that last part sure isn't hard to do, is it? Ha-ha-ha.

Hey, baldy!

Hey cueball! Anybody ever tell you that your head looks like an 8-ball?

Hey, pinhead! Wanna go bowling?

I've never seen a bowling ball with eyes before!

You get the idea.

Hey, at least I'm trying to cope with it. I could just go back to bed, curl up under the blanket with my kitty cat, and call it a day.

But that wouldn't be any fun now, would it?

Nope.

So...I sit down at my trusty old Acer laptop and type away, learning to laugh at myself.

It's all I can do.

#

So...I type and laugh at how silly this all is, me worried about some hair – that will eventually grow back with time – and how silly I've been to place so much emphasis on something as trivial as some hair.

Something that means so little, as opposed to who and what I am on the *inside*, not the outside.

It has been said that beauty is only skin deep, and I sincerely believe that. You can be so attractive on the outside, but so ugly on the outside, or vice-versa.

Your outward appearance means absolutely nothing compared to a good heart and soul, to be loving and kind to others.

Just like deep down, I'm a good man, no matter how much weight I lose or hair or how pale my skin may look for now.

So...I sit here and type away and laugh at all of this, and move on with my day.

I have more important things to think about for tomorrow.

FORTY FOUR

December 18th, 2023, early morning.

Well, one hour and fifteen minutes to chemo.

Hair was still coming out this morning.

Not a good way to start the day, but, hey, at least I'll have something to joke about while I'm there.

Hey, cueball is here! The bowling ball with eyes! Here comes old baldy!

It's better than being depressed the whole time I'm there, right?

I think so.

So...off I go!

#

It's not too bad in here. In the infusion center.

While I'm getting "infused" I have a TV set, books to read, and even snacks if I get hungry. There is a big bay window to look out of when the sun is shining. It could be worse.

But it could be better.

I could be at home, in familiar surroundings, watching my TV and petting my kitty.

But, first things first.

My old buddy, Mr Chemo.

My constant companion.
My constant reminder of how sick I am.
Time to go kick the Big C's butt.

FORTY FIVE

December 19th, 2023, early morning.

Well, yesterday wasn't too bad.

I spent my time in the chemo infusion center eating some decent food, watching TV, and reading a book. Quiet and peaceful. At least I have a good atmosphere to look forward to over there.

Another thing I like about it, is that there are other people there for the same reason; fighting the Big C.

We are all there for each other, to share our stories and feel a little better, anyway, and anyone who has been through this knows that a little better is better than nothing.

And so it goes.

#

Today I'm feeling a little "woozy," but otherwise not too bad. Like all other feelings these days, it just comes with the territory.

As you can see, I'm sitting at my trusty old Acer laptop again, typing away, recording more of my current journey with the Big C. My battle.

My life line to the world. To my feeling of normalcy. To just another day in the life of a man who has nothing left to lose except his life, who intends to go down fighting tooth and nail until the bitter end.

Come hell or high water, I intend to beat the Big C at it's own game.

Or, die trying.

Amen.

FORTY SIX

December 22nd, 2023, early morning.

Another day, just me and my constant companion, my chemo pack.

The tubing coming from the pack is now so tangled up, I'm afraid the chemo juice won't flow correctly, so now I'm sitting here, in vain, trying to untangle it. They should issue an instruction manual with these damn things. Ha-ha.

Otherwise, not a bad day. Yet, that is.

This round of chemo, since the onocologist has decided to cut the strength down about thirty percent, has actually been easier to handle as far as the nausea, dizziness, and other side effects are concerned.

Cool by me!

Not that I'm in the position to be too choosy, mind you, but even a small break in the side effects is always welcome. I can actually concentrate, enjoy my creature comforts when I'm feeling less stressed out and feeling less pain and discomfort.

Keeping my fingers crossed!

#

Now, to untangle this damn tubing, ha-ha.

I've never seen such a mess. What I can't figure out is, how am I expected to untangle this tubing if the business end of it leads directly to my chemo pump?

Good question...

No plausible solution.

Help!

#

Well, I got the tubing untangled, but now the pack strap is all tangled up.

Help!

Ha-ha.

No matter! At two pm today, I bid farewell to my chemo pack for two weeks! Yippee!

But for now, time to untangle my pack strap and move on with the day.

See ya tomorrow!

FORTY SEVEN

December 23rd, 2023, early morning.

Two days until Christmas, and the side effects from the chemo are already kicking in; sore throat, headache, the usual crap.

I should have known.

The old fickled bitch again, the Big C, working wonders for my health and general attitude.

Also on the current agenda; weak, blurry eyes, lack of balance, dizziness.

I just feel like *poop*.

Oh well. Back to the usual routine.

I sit down at my trusty old Acer laptop, and share my current feelings with the world.

#

Not to be so depressing, mind you, but more to help those other unfortunate folks out there, who may be going through the same thing right now, and are beginning to feel lost, all alone, and worst of all, maybe losing the faith.

Please, don't do that.

Remember; sometimes, hope – and faith – are all we have left.

Believe me, I know.

All too well.

But, it comes with the territory. I was just hoping I'd feel better on Christmas – on our Lord Christ's birthday – than I'm feeling right now, that's all.

Then again, it's up to me – and all of us – to decide how we may feel on any given day. Christmas should be no different.

If we sit around on Christmas, feeling sorry and negative and sad, that's exactly how we'll feel all day, and on Christ's birthday. Do you think he would want us to just give up, feel this way on such a special day?

Of course not. He would want us to celebrate this day, and be glad for it. Be positive.

Keep the faith.

Just like I'm going to try and do today, no matter how hard it may be.

It's all I have left.

That's what I used to think, anyway.

FORTY EIGHT

December 24th, 2023, mid- morning.

As of this morning, I'm beginning to feel somewhat differently about the situation.

I imagine that by now, I'm beginning to sound like a broken record; positive one day, negative the next day. Blah-blah-blah.

But today, I'm going to start looking at the situation more logically, and begin looking at each day like it's a gift.

Which it is.

But, first things first.

To face the cold, hard truth before moving on.

#

I have *cancer.*

I may have it *forever* – it may take my life someday.

I don't know what the future holds for me – yet.

So...why wake up each day, feeling as though my day may *be* or may *not* be a good one, every day, and torture myself this way?

I should wake up each and every day, no matter how I feel, being thankful that God has graced me with yet another day on this beautiful Earth, and move on to the next day and the next, being glad for something I used to take for granted until now.

Yes, I know this may sound like a very difficult task for those of you who may be in the same position I'm in right now, but it needs to be done, not only for your sake, but your loved one's sake as well.

Your friends and loved ones need to see you live every day with a positive attitude. See a smile on your face and a twinkle in your eye. If you do pass away someday, if the Big C does get the best of you, they will be left with some pleasant memories of how strong you were, fighting the good fight, and smiling the while time you were fighting.

You owe it to *yourself.*

Before it's too late.

#

So, beginning on Christmas day, on December 25th, 2023, I, myself, am turning over a new leaf, as the old saying goes.

No more waking up feeling bad – which is only normal under the circumstances – and doing my level best to stay that way all day long. Feel sorry for myself, and focusing on how unfair life has been to me.

No more sob stories posted on social media. No more gloomy days made worse by concentrating on only the bad things.

No more being the old me, and only being the new me. The *new* David.

The strong one, who always goes down fighting, and is grateful for the opportunity.

Amen.

#

So now, my new day begins.

My new life.

On today's agenda; bake some good cookies for Christmas day. Maybe some good bread, too, like pumpkin or banana.

Or a pie.

Who knows?

The possibilities are endless, with the right attitude.

Or, maybe I'll just sit back and watch TV and pet my kitty cat and take a well deserved nap.

Who knows? Maybe I will do *all* of these things, make a whole day of it.

Besides, tomorrow is Christmas, and I have an important birthday to celebrate. The birth of the being that has made my life as it is, possible.

My *second chance* at life.

Yes...I think tomorrow is going to be a good day.

FORTY NINE

December 25th, 2023, Christmas morning.

Merry Christmas!

Today, as I sit here at my computer on Christmas morning, my mind drifts back to holiday seasons of the past few years, and having to say a sad farewell to some old friends.

In 2018, an old friend of mine, George, passed away from a *long* battle with several different types of cancer, and he didn't have a good time doing so, either.

To be honest, I don't know how he did it.

He had parts of his body, on the inside, removed, that should *not* have been removed. He had cancer in places that you wouldn't think cancer would even touch.

He endured this for many, *many* years too. More years than any one man or human being in general should ever have to endure. He endured it until he was skeletal, ghostly pale, and withering away to nothing.

Point being?

He *did endure*.

Old George endured more pain and misery and heartache than anyone should ever have to endure, and then some. I'd imagine, at one point during all of this suffering, he wanted to give up and *die*.

Throw in the proverbial towel. Give up the fight, and admit defeat.

But he didn't.

He fought the good fight, and kept on fighting until he took his last breath.

Just like I, myself, must do now.

#

I've had quite a few friends die from cancer and other horrible diseases over the last thirty years or so, and it never gets easier.

Although I am definitely no stranger to the subject of death, the news of George's passing hit me *hard*.

Over the last 25 years, I have said goodbye to countless old friends who have passed on way too young. I have been a pallbearer for several of them. I have found a dead body in a motel room {I worked there at the time as a maintenance man} and I spent almost five years watching my own Father sit in a chair and slowly wither away until he mercifully passed on.

One would think that these experiences would toughen me up, *harden* me to the subject of death. Not so. All it did for me was to make me feel sick, empty, and depressed. Does being around death make you a tough guy? Not really. Far from it, actually.

In all honesty? It just made me wonder just how long I may have left on this Earth.

Well, I guess that question may have been answered, huh?

Maybe.

Or...maybe not.

Maybe I'll just take George's example, and run with it.

Be brave in the face of death, and fight that good fight, and the whole time wearing a big smile, and telling cancer it has picked the wrong guy to pick on now, and it better be ready for one hell of a battle, because I sure as hell am.

Thank you, George, not only for your bravery in the face of such enormous odds being against you, but for your invalauble friendship way back when as well.

You are still missed by us all, and always will be. How can we all not admire and respect and remember such bravery?

Amen.

FIFTY

December 26th, 2023, late morning.

Well, here I am again, sitting at my trusty old Acer laptop, sharing my most recent adventures with you – for better or worse.

Today, I woke up with small, blister-like sores on both my upper and lower lip, which of course makes it harder to eat now more than ever.

Just what I didn't need.

But, as I've said before, if you don't keep the faith, fight the good fight, you will only make matters worse for yourself.

So, I carry on.

#

I've got a refill on my Magic Mouthwash and MuGuard, so the pain will be at least somewhat less severe when I eat. The trick is, how you *angle* the food as you put it in your mouth.

For example; when I eat pudding, I use a *small* spoon, and scoop up some pudding, turning the spoon *upside down* as I place it in my mouth. For some odd reason, it works as far as the severity of the pain is concerned, so I stick with whatever works for me.

Another example of how to lessen the pain while drinking, is to use a drinking straw, and taking only *small* sips each time.

Believe me, once you've been through this type of pain and discomfort, your mind will come up with all sorts of ways to ease your pain – even if only briefly.

Briefly is *way better* than nothing at all.

Keep the faith, fight that good fight.

Sometimes, it's all you can do.

#

One of the most distressing but yet eye opening things I've learned about cancer is, it is relentless in it's nature.

Without a good fight, of the heart and human spirit, you don't stand a chance of beating it at it's own game. Cancer knows no boundaries when it comes to inflicting pain or injury. It has no concept of right or wrong or empathy.

It is not real, in the human sense. It is not a living being capable of guilt or remorse. It is just a nasty little demon that does it best to kill you, and seems to relish in that idea, as if it has a mind of it's own.

You cannot reason with it or beg for mercy or change it's mind. It is here for a purpose, and one purpose only.

To make your life a living hell until you mercifully die.

That's why you have to keep the faith, and fight the good fight.

Amen.

FIFTY ONE

December 27th, 2023, late morning.

Today, I thought I'd focus on something more positive.

My readers are probably thinking, *Positive?! Is he sick?*

Well, yes, I have cancer folks. Gotta remain positive at least *part* of the time.

So, today, I am focusing on things to brighten up my day.

First, I look in the mirror, to see I have lost more hair, right above my temple. My head is beginning to resemble a not-so-well-made bird nest. All that's missing are the bird eggs.

I think, oh well, at least I am a low maintenance groomer now, huh?

I move on to shaving.

#

Well, that was exciting. What's next on the agenda for today?

Ah...yes, breakfast.

I think I'll have cream of wheat today. Something healthy. *Gotta beat the Big C's ass!*

Top it off with some orange juice and toast, and yum yum! I couldn't really taste it, but at least it was healthy.

Now, for my next trick, I will log into my computer and work on my book! Oh, wait, you already know that.

Exciting, huh?

Hey, at least it is *positive*.

I have learned recently that at least one positive thought or action per day makes one feel better. Making something positive out of something negative. Taking a seemingly hopeless situation and making it hopeful.

Each day I am graced by God with waking up to spend another day on this beautiful planet, I give thanks not only by working on my book, but also by just giving thanks in general for the things I *do* have.

For example, today, I was able to eat my breakfast without any severe pain, which is different from yesterday. I was able to comb what hair I have left, groom myself, without any trouble.

When you have cancer, each day that you wake up being able to use the bathroom by yourself, groom yourself, cook your own meals, etc., is a major accomplishment, and should be appreciated and celebrated.

POSITIVE.

There lies the key to success.

Positivity.

Without it? You may as well stay in bed, wipe your poor little snotty nose, and give up.

I, myself, don't intend to do so.

FIFTY TWO

December 28th, 2023, late morning.

Today is another day to celebrate!

Today is the day I get my book royalty payments deposited in the bank. It probably won't be much, but it's money, right?

Positivity.

And more money for pudding and ice cream!

Yeah, this cancer still has me on a "soft food" diet. But, that also means I can eat a lot of sweet goodies too!

Soft chocolate, soft cookies, and donuts!

I was told to keep my calorie intake pretty steady for now, because I lost twenty five pounds in less than three weeks. *Not* good.

But things could be worse.

I could be immobile, and hooked up to a feeding tube. I could be bedridden and virtually helpless.

See?

Positivity.

With each and every positive step you take, the closer you come to inner peace. Believe me, when you are fighting the Big C, you need all of the inner peace you can get.

Therefore, positivity.

Now, on with my day.

#

It's snowing outside today, which doesn't really thrill me too much.

I had planned for at least a small amount of outside activity today – rake some leaves, etc. - but now I won't be doing anything but sitting in front of the TV, I guess.

I mean, that's okay, but TV sure isn't what it used to be. Having grown up in the baby boomer generation, a lot of the TV shows I see now are...well, rotten.

For example, the cartoons.

The Flintstones, The Jetsons, Scooby Doo, and my favorite cartoons, the classic Warner Brother's cartoons, which featured Bugs Bunny, Daffy Duck, Wiley Coyote, The Roadrunner, Elmer Fudd, Sylvester the cat and Tweety Bird, and Foghorn Leghorn.

When I was a kid, I could sit there for hours on end and watch those classic cartoons, and never get tired of them. In those days, cartoons were not only very funny, but also squeaky clean, harmless fun for kids to watch.

Not so as time went on.

Now days, not so. Since the 90s, we have had a whole *breed* of so called cartoons to choose from, which include Ren and Stimpy – a dog and cat who would {attempt} to entertain you by walking around with snot dripping from their nose, consuming boogers, farting, burping, and generally just being as gross and offensive as possible.

Next up was Beavis & Butthead, who, in all aspects, were nothing more than a couple of dumb, crude, mindless, ugly, sexist, self-destructive fools.

One particular episode in it's first season dealt with a juvenile obsession with arson, which, after watching the episode, prompted five-year-old Austin Messner of Moraine, Ohio, to set his Mother's home on fire, killing his younger sister in the process. I guess he thought fire was funny – in typical Beavis and Butthead fashion, that is.

See what I mean? Whether it be a cartoon or a TV show, things have not changed for the better.

Still, at the same time, with all of the new streaming channels and Netflix and different cable packages available these days, a person, regardless of what era they grew up in, can find something to watch that suits their fancy.

When you are in my shoes, locked up in your home without anything to do at any given time, other than the "same old routine," believe me, you will stop looking a gift horse in the mouth and appreciate what you do have to occupy your time.

Just saying.

So...on with the day!

FIFTY THREE

December 31st, 2023, New Year's Eve

Yesterday, I had been reflecting back on the days when my journey with the Big C had just begun, and all of the mixed emotions that I had felt during those dark days.

So, I wrote down my feelings to share them with other cancer patients in hopes that it might help them cope with their feelings in a more positive way.

I call this story, "My Own Little Demon," which I am quite sure any seasoned cancer survivor can relate to.

#

I live with a demon.

It's there, every day, with me 24-7, keeping me company, as it continues to torture me by invading my heart, my soul, my very being.

It tempts me with things that I shouldn't do or say. It wants me to give in to these temptations, further my rapid decline into my own personal madness.

My own little demon, it *loves* me, you see.

It loves me in a way no other has ever loved me. It loves me rain or shine, good or bad. It loves me so much, it is willing to spend every last second of it's miserable existence making sure I'm just as miserable as it is.

Misery really does love company, I guess.

#

My little demon, it loves me so much, just the other day it told me I should go down to the local package store, pick me up a bottle of cheap booze, and cure the pain in my heart and guts that eats away at me every day, like a cancer.

It knows I have been sober for almost seventeen years, but it wants me to ruin my sobriety for the sake of my sanity.

For the sake of my health.

It knows that if I do so, I'll be even more miserable than I am already, but it is doing so in my best interests, you know?

It loves me.

It only wants the best for me. Who else would tempt me to slowly but surely kill myself, but someone who really cares, and is willing to join me in my own personal journey into my own private hell?

My own little demon, of course.

Just the other day, it told me I should go to the store and buy a carton of cigarettes, when it knows I'm trying to quit. Was I offended by such a crazy idea? Of course not.

My little demon would never ask me to do anything it wouldn't be willing to do, too.

Yeah...it loves me.

#

Who else but my own little demon would ask me to eat high calorie, sugar infused breakfast cereal instead of something healthy? Who else would tempt with candy and ice cream and pudding and other creature comforts, but my own little demon?

The one who wants the best for me, and is always right there, suffering with me, for better or worse.

In sickness and in bad health, ubntil death do us part?

My little demon, that's who.

Who else would wake me up each day, feeling like walking death already, my mind and heart and very soul filled with my own personal demons already, yet sacrifices it's time to make sure I'm taken care of?

You know who.

Why, just this morning, it told me I should just stay in bed, lay around all day, not even shower or shave or eat or give a damn about anything that might make me feel more human again.

That's right, it says, in a voice that sounds eerily like my own voice. *Just stay in bed, don't even move. Don't even breathe. Just lay there like a worthless, lazy pile of human waste and GIVE UP.*

But don't worry, I'll be right there with you!

Yes, I know.

Until death do us part.

#

Just today, as I was watching TV, it told me I should stop watching my favorite TV shows {true crime, documentaries, non-fictional content} and watch low class reality shows, shows with sex and nudity and foul language, something that will eat up what few brain cells I have left.

That's where I draw the line, though.

I have to have at least something left that my little demon has no say-so over, so I tell it NO.

In return for my bold decision, my little demon makes me feel like hell all day long; sore throat, aches and pains, and fills my tired mind full of ghastly visions of what terrible things could happen to me if I don't comply with it's wishes.

But it loves me.

Who else would stick by me through it all?

My own little demon, that's who.

#

But as my day went on, I didn't feel so lucky any more, to have my own little demon by my side.

Slowly but surely, all of the feelings of love and devotion for me faded away, and were replaced by deep rooted feelings of hopelessness, loneliness, and desperation.

I felt all *alone*.

It was as though my own little demon, in an act of anger and betrayal, had decided I wasn't worth it's dedication to me, and left me behind to suffer all alone.

It was then I realized that my own little demon I thought I would always be by my side, really loved me, had so cruelly left me behind to rot in my own sickness and misery.

It was also then that I realized that my own little demon, the one I had thought was there with me 24-7, wasn't real at all.

Just a figment of my own imagination. Wishful thinking. One last grasp at some sense of normalcy. A way to explain such a crazy thought without admitting to myself that maybe, just *maybe*, if I didn't start facing my own sad reality, I'd go insane from it all.

So I closed my eyes, clasped my hands together, and prayed.

A prayer to the REAL best friend I had in the world. The only REAL savior.

My God.

From that moment on, after admitting I was losing grasp on my own life, and asked for his foregivness, I felt like a new man.

Had a new lease on life.

My little demon still comes to visit me every day, but I know how to handle it now.

After all, my cancer – my own little demon – isn't going away until I face my own demons head on, and move forward with my only real savior by my side. My little demon didn't really love me, anway. It was just there to remind me of how miserable I was, and wanted me to give up. Take my life.

But I won't let it fool me any more.

I found my true path now, and I don't need any

nasty little demons to help me.
I have GOD on my side.
Amen.

FIFTY FOUR

January 1ˢᵗ, 2024 / early morning

Happy New Year!

It may be a new year, but I don't feel very new myself. Ha-ha.

I feel like the same sick old fart as always. Then again, God blessed me with yet another day on this beautiful Earth, so I can't complain too much.

Positivity.

This morning, though, I did notice that I am starting to lose my sense of smell and taste. Mostly my sense of taste. I had cream of wheat for breakfast, dosed with some maple syrup and a dab of peanut butter, and I might as well have been eating cardboard with some peanut butter on it.

Not good.

I know by now that I am always going to have side effects with my chemo, but I would like to enjoy what little food I do eat.

Oh well...on with the day.

#

As I sat watching the local news channel today {which I very rarely do, because all I ever see is *bad* news} I noticed one thing above all; our society had seemed to forgotten that God even exists.

Which also brought to mind, why is it that so many of us – myself included in the past – don't even think about God, or speak to him, unless they are in dire need of something?

I've been guilty of this too, in recent weeks, on those days I felt so overwhelmed with pain and hopelessness. Instead of feeling lucky to be alive, I felt angry, and didn't even think about the fact that it was God who had graced me with another day on Earth, and I should be thankful for it.

Then, to make matters worse, when I did speak to God, it was solely for the reason of self preservation.

Dear Lord, please let this pain stop! Please, God, make me better! Heal me! Perform a miracle for me!

But on the days I didn't feel as bad as others, the last thing on my mind was speaking to God.

Sad, isn't it?

Now, don't get me wrong; I'm not saying that all folks who have been through these same mixed emotions are bad people, or don't believe in God. I'm merely saying that at times, and it is usually the worst times in our lives, we don't seem to appreciate what we do have, and only focus on ourselves and our own problems, instead of feeling blessed for what we do have.

The things that GOD gave us.

I know it's only human nature, in a time of extreme distress – cancer being one of them – to feel somewhat self centered, but we all have to eventually open our eyes to what's going on around us, like... being lucky enough to wake up again.

You remember God, right?

If not? I suggest you do so in the future, before it's too late. Start out the new year being thankful for what we have.

Just saying.

FIFTY FIVE

January 2nd, 2024 / early morning

My taste buds are still numb, can't taste much of anything unless it's hot or spicy, but otherwise, I'm still hanging in there.

I even thought about adding chili powder or diced peppers to my oatmeal, but after thinking it over, I decided that was a little too extreme. Ha-ha.

One good thing; I did manage to find some inexpensive sleep aid tablets that help me sleep better at night, which I really needed. Sometimes the after effects of the chemo tend to make me toss and turn at night, and I wake up feeling even more drained than before.

That's one thing you can count on with the Big C. For each and every positive thing you accomplish, there is at least one {or more} negative aspect involved in the situation.

But...as usual, I must persevere, move on with my day, and try to find something positive in all of the mess I have to work with.

So...I write!

#

It's only five days until chemo again.

In an odd way, I'm looking forward to it. I mean, I am looking forward to having the chemo in me again, eating away at the cancer cells, shrinking them down and making them go away.

Recently, someone I know that has been through chemo several times, told me that you never *really* get rid of cancer. Or the after effects of chemo. That's why it's called "remission" instead of being told you are *cured*.

In other words, once you have had cancer, there is always going to be a little bit of it left inside you somewhere, just biding it's time, waiting to flare up again at any moment, and maybe win the battle this time, and take your life.

Not a very pleasant thought, but nothing I'm not used to by now.

So, I move on with my day, and try to make the best of it, and stay positive.

It's all I can do.

FIFTY SIX

January 4th, 2024 / early morning

Three days until chemo.

Here comes the feelings of uneasiness again, the bad thoughts. The dread.

Yet, at the same time, a feeling of relief, of knowing that I will have something coarsing through my veins that could help me reach that often times unreachable plateau; *remission.*

Mixed emotions.

Positivity.

But I have to walk that line, without teetering over the edge.

I close my eyes, take a deep breath, exhale, and move on with my day.

#

My sense of smell and taste are still going all wonky on me, but at least I still have them to a certain extent, which in my case is better than nothing.

My hearing has been effected too, which is weird. I can hear but people have to raise their voice another octave or two for me to understand them. I have no inner ear infection, so the loss of hearing doesn't make any sense. Better call the doctor again.

Same old crap, just different day.

Positivity!

Yeah...I know.

Never give up.

And turn up the volume on my TV. Ha-ha.

#

As you can see, I'm working on the book again.

It's coming along quite well, if I say so myself. Very informative, yet kinda depressing too. But, as I've said before, not only does it come with the territory, but it also deals with cancer, you know?

Hard to sugarcoat a turd.

But I'm doing my best. Ha-ha.

I really hope this book helps others, too. Help them along their journey with the Big C, and beyond.

Beyond all of their bad dreams and fears and to that beautiful place known as remission, and then, someday, beyond the golden gates of Heaven where they will never have to suffer again.

Just like me, and my own journey. Who better than a man who is fighting the Big C with all the strength he can muster to guide others along their own journey?

But for now, this tired old fart is going to take a break, eat breakfast, and watch some TV. Pet my kitty cat. Wash some dishes. Hey, at least I'm still strong enough to do so.

But I will be back soon, to share some more of my journey with you, and you can share your own journey someday, too.

Until then, take care.

Hope.

Pray.

Never give up.

It's all we can do, isn't it?

Amen.

FIFTY SEVEN

January 5th, 2024 / early morning

Today is grocery store day!

More ice cream and pudding and other tasty treats for me to enjoy before chemo starts again!

It's really weird how I was told by a doctor to eat more calorie infused food items, but I don't care. Fine by me. I just figured sugar wouldn't be good for a cancer patient, but I'm not going to argue with my doctor! Ha-ha.

My sense of taste and smell are still off a bit, but not enough to ruin my day.

So...on to the store!

#

Well, that wasn't good.

When I was walking through the store, I felt sort of dizzy, almost fainted. Needless to say, I cut my shopping trip short.

This damn cancer, it tends to pop up when I least expect it, in some way or another. But I hate it when it decides to pop up in the public eye.

Not that my condition is anything to be ashamed of, mind you, but I tend to find it somewhat embarrassing at times. It makes me feel awkward, I guess, to be seen in public walking around like a zombie.

Or those really embarrassing times when I'm standing in line at the store, and the checkout lady says *are you okay? You don't look so good.*

I shouldn't feel embarrassed, but I do. I know it was just a fellow human being showing concern for a regular customer, but I still felt like I was being put on the spot, like everyone within earshot was *staring* at me, like they were afraid that whatever was wrong with me was contagious, and they would be infected if they got too close to me.

I feel like a walking *germ*.

Silly, of course, but you would be surprised what goes through your mind in my position.

But, I just try my best to shrug it off, and go on with my day. It's all I can do.

So, on with my day; it's time for ice cream and pudding and Netflix!

FIFTY EIGHT

January 6th, 2024 / early morning

Well, another cloudy, gloomy day.

Chance of snow in the forecast, too. It seems like after I ended up with cancer, something as simple as a cloudy Winter day makes me even more depressed.

Not good.

Today, I woke up graced with stomach cramps, constipation, and a headache. Then I look out the window to see a lousy day, and wanted to roll back over and fall asleep.

But, I knew I couldn't do that.

That would be admitting defeat, and I can't allow the Big C to defeat me. Not today, or any other day, for that matter.

When I wake up to yet another gloomy day, that's when I have to fight the good fight *twice* as hard, and defeat the gloomy feeling that threatens to defeat me again. It's always there, rain or shine, warm or cold, day or night.

My constant companion.

The Big C.

The gloomy little demon that wants me to give up, sign off the computer, and lay back down in bed and fall asleep and waste the day away like a coward.

155

But, I'm not going to give it the satisfaction.

Because I am a true *survivor.*

If I wasn't, I wouldn't be sitting here typing away and planning to eat ice cream and watch TV and telling the Big C to buzz off.

Positivity.

Keeping the faith.

Hope and prayer.

Fighting the good fight.

Amen.

#

The hits just keep on coming.

I found out this morning that my insurance company is still refusing to pay for my Magic Wash and Muguard {things I need for then pain in my mouth and throat} which means next week, after I come off of chemo again, I'll have nothing to combat the side effects.

Nice huh?

Not really, considering that I have always paid my dues with my insurance company, only to have them abandon me when I need them the most.

In addition, I have also found out that my Senior Food Stamp card has been cut down by eight dollars, when I only had fifty-six dollars a month as it was.

I guess anyone past the age of fifty-five is considered a dinosaur in our society, and won't be around much longer to take from the rich, so we just don't matter.

Oh well, on with my day.

#

There was one bright spot in my day, though.

Also included in my mail today was a small package – with no name or return address – that contained a couple of do-rags – bandanas – to wear over my balding head.

Included with the package was a note that read:

Have a great day, David. I care!
You are in my prayers.

Now, how could I not feel lucky – and most of all, blessed – after receiving such a gift right out of the blue?

Now I finally realize that I am *not* all alone in the world. There *is* someone out there who cares. Each day I sit here all alone, I'm not really alone at all.

Just when I needed something – or someone – the most, I received this gift.

A coincidence?

I think not.

I think this was meant to be, and, also by divine intervention. I believe that God let this person know how badly I was in need of something positive in my life, therefore I received it.

That's what I think. So, to whoever you are that brightened up my day, I say thank you so much, and I hope to meet you face to face someday to thank you in person.

Amen.

FIFTY NINE

January 7th, 2024 / early morning

Tomorrow is chemo day.

My *third* round of chemo within just a few weeks, as a matter of fact - and believe me, I feel it.

The Big C, that is.

Still coarsing through my upper body like a freight train, my one way ticket to Hell on Earth.

I can feel it in my throat, still fighting the chemo with all it can muster. Eating away at me. Wanting me to give up, and lay down, and *die*.

But the Big C doesn't know who it's messing with this time. I didn't start writing this book just to quit writing it and lay down and give up.

I, myself – and this book – are still here for a reason.

So, I move on wth my day.

#

So far, other than some discomfort in my mouth and throat, I feel decent for a change.

That's one thing about this whole process I'll never get used to; each time I go through this, I'm just beginning to feel half way human again, and it's right back to the chemo.

It almost doesn't seem fair, does it? I know by now that life isn't always fair, but, you would think I would get a break at least every now and then.

That's the Big C for you; the gift that keeps on giving, whether you need it or not.

Remember; *positivity.*

Keep the faith. Hope and pray.

Fight the good fight.

Amen.

SIXTY

January 8th, 2024 / early morning

Chemo day; countdown, two hours and twenty-eight minutes until the big event.

The Big C injection.

My lifeline to remission.

My constant companion.

I hope it's working.

#

Well, that wasn't too bad.

I had a decent lunch; soup and crackers and spring water and dessert. And so far, no nausea or upset stomach.

Today I brought my cell phone and headphones and a book to read, and I'm just sitting here relaxing and waiting for my Keytruda infusion. At least I have a decent chair to sit in and I'm kicking back, chilling out before the main event...the *chemo!*

My constant companion!

My best buddy.

Now, let's not be too sarcastic, it may be helping you for all you know.

Positivity!

That's the ticket!

So, I lean back, close my eyes, take a deep breath, exhale, and turn it all over to God.

He is my constant companion, too, you see; always there, watching over me, making sure his plan for me is carried out someday.

I'm anxious to see just what his plan may be, too. I hope it's better than this.

I hope I get to finish this book.

I hope.

SIXTY ONE

January 9th, 2024 / early morning

Well, that was interesting – but not in a good way.

My little gadget that infuses me with my chemo juice stopped working last night – right about bedtime, of course – and began making an annoying beeping sound that would have kept me awake all night.

So I had to take the batteries out and have to call for a replacement today. And I'm going to be at least 14 hours behind on my treatment process.

It comes with the territory.

#

Back from the chemo center.

It was a kink in the line that caused the gadget to shut down. Once the kink was stretched so far, it cut off the flow of the chemo, thus the beeping sound to warn me of the problem.

But, after the kink was straightened out, and some brand new batteries were installed, it's working like a charm.

Funny, isn't it? How you absolutely hate chemo, yet, when you think you aren't getting your chemo, you freak out and worry about what could be life saving drugs being blocked from your body, that could save your life?

Mixed emotions for sure, but no matter what, you end up wanting that chemo in the end. I know; it's a weird feeling, but quite natural for someone in my position.

A man fighting the good fight.

A man who wants to be a *true survivor.*

So...on with my day, whatever it may bring.

#

So far, it has brought me a good show on Netflix, a good cheeseburger, and some very tasty French vanilla ice cream.

What else could a man in my position ask for?

Amen.

SIXTY TWO

January 10th, 2024 / early morning

Today is social security check day! Yippee!

My favorite day of the month; more grocery shopping, and this month, I thought I'd buy myself a new pair of blue jeans and some new shoes.

A guy in my position has to treat himself to some mild luxuries now and then, right? Why not!

That's another thing I've learned from my battle with cancer; live each and every day like there's no tomorrow, and enjoy it to it's fullest while you have the chance. If a new pair of jeans or a pair of Walmart shoes makes you feel better, so be it.

Of course, I have to have my creature comforts as well; my ice cream, banana bread, and my other tasty snacks.

This guy intends to *enjoy* what life he has left. That way, if cancer does end up winning the battle, I didn't allow it to ruin what days I had left.

I fought the good fight, and won all of the daily battles until then.

Amen.

#

Well, Walmart was a crazy place today.

Whenever I walk in there, and glance around, it seems like an army of ants scurrying all around, running into each other searching for that next great deal, which there are none of, at today's prices.

So I just move on through the crowd, trying to ignore all of the lunacy going on around me, and go about my business.

In all honesty, I can see why the folks around me seem so nervous and fidgety; it is hard to find a bargain there days; inflation is still running rampant at our local retail stores, and there seems to be no end in sight.

But I try my best to look at it this way; in my current state of mind and health, I still feel lucky to be able to afford anything I need, and just try to be thankful for what I have.

Positivity.

Don't let anyone or anything get you down.

Amen.

SIXTY THREE

January 11th, 2024 / early morning

Well, I woke up today with the pain in my mouth and throat kicking in again.

It never fails, two days *before* I get off chemo, the pain and discomfort are already kicking in again. It never seems to fail; I'm not away from partial relief for very long before I'm not.

It goes with the territory. Yes, I know.

Positivity.

Just move on.

#

Speaking of moving on, I wanted to share this with you, a painting I saw on the wall of the waiting room of the onocology office.

It is entitled "What cancer *cannot* do," and it speaks volumes as to the strength of the human spirit.

Below is the text from the painting:

Cancer cannot cripple love.

It cannot shatter hope.

It cannot corrode faith.

It cannot destroy peace.
It cannot kill friendship.
It cannot suppress your memories.
It cannot silence courage.
It cannot invade the soul.
It cannot steal eternal life.
It cannot conquer the human spirit.
Amen.

SIXTY FOUR

January 12th, 2024 / early morning

I'm glad I get off chemo today.

I'm going to spend the day relaxing and spend the weekend celebrating.

I don't mean to sound like a big baby, but this last round of chemo really got me down; constipation, stomach cramps, fever, mouth and throat pain.

Yes...I *know*.

It comes with the territory...and remember:

It cannot shatter hope.

It cannot corrode faith.

It cannot conquer the human spirit.

Amen.

#

At certain times, whether you like it or not, you do have to reflect back on your past to appreciate the future.

For example, I have had some terrible things happen to me over the last fifteen years or so. I had my left thumb crushed off at work {the doctors were able to graft it back on, so that was a good thing} but it was a horrible injury, and left me jobless at the time.

At the age of 58, after over a decade of being single, I thought I'd met a lady who was the perfect one for me, even bought her an engagement ring, only to find out the hard way she wasn't exactly the faithful type.

Yes, I know; affairs of the heart are different than affairs of the health, but, at times, they seem to fit all too well together in one big gut-punch.

A simple word or action on the part of another can be almost debilitating to the very heart and soul of one that is already damaged or broken spiritually. Point being, I have had enough disappointment and sickness and heartache over the last decade or so to end up like this.

Yet I move on.

It's all I can do.

It cannot conquer the human spirit.

Yes, I know.

I've come this far, have suffered too much, to allow anything – including the Big C – to stop me now.

Plus, I always have *God* on my side.

What more could I ask for?

So, today, I will begin yet another day in my long journey, hopefully back to a state of better health, both physically and spiritually, and just keep the faith.

Amen.

Part 4
My Journey Comes To An End

SIXTY FIVE

January 13th, 2024 / early morning

As of today, I have seventeen days until my next – and hopefully *last* – round of chemo.

Then, sometime in early February, I go back for a Pet scan to see if the chemo has set me on the road to remission – or not.

I have to admit, the feeling of uneasiness is setting in again, which I'm sure is normal, under the circumstances, yet I feel *a lot* more uneasy this time. I guess it's the terrible side effects I dealt with on my third round of chemo, but regardless of what is making me feel this way, it's not very reassuring.

So...it's back to my computer {as you can see} and onward to a better day – I hope.

I guess we'll see, won't we?

#

You know, the most silly ideas can cross your mind when you're on chemo.

For example; after I climbed out of the shower this morning, looking at myself in the mirror, my general appearance made me feel so sad.

I'm almost completely bald on top, my hairline receded and thin, turning grey. The skin on my face and neck is pale and wrinkled, and the pallor of my skin is nothing more than of a ghost of who I used to be.

An empty shell of a man.

A dead man walking.

My whole body racked with pain and emptiness, the chemo having dried me up like an old prune inside and out.

I almost cried.

Then, I thought to myself, *what is wrong with you? You can't help the way you look. Why don't you stop feeling sorry for yourself, and do something about it?*

So...I began my "home makeover."

#

Believe me, fellas, makeovers aren't just for the ladies these days.

Especially if you are a chemo patient.

As I looked into the mirror at myself, I thought, why not shave? The hair on your face is still growing. Why not dry shampoo your hair, and comb it back?

Use some eyedrops to clear up those tired, bleary eyes? Brush what teeth you have left. Shed those wrinkled old Pjs and dress in some decent clothing.

A full *makeover.*

That's the ticket!

So, a makeover it is.

#

There, that's better.

Now I look and feel human again – or, about as human as a person can feel under these circumstances – and I do feel better than I did before, ready to face the world and whatever it may have in store for me today.

Then, as I sit down at my computer again to work on my book, another revelation about my current situation hits me like a bolt right out of the blue; why was I worried about all of this in the first place?

As I sit looking at my reflection in my computer screen, I think, even if you hadn't had a makeover, do you actually believe that anyone that really cares about you – family, friends, etc. - would really care about your new appearance? Look down upon you for looking this way?

Feel awkward or embarrassed by the way you look? Feel repulsed or saddened by it?

No, of course not.

They would do their best to understand and be kind to you, regardless of your appearance.

Point being, if you want to have a makeover, for YOU, to make yourself feel better, go for it. But don't ever believe that your friends and loved ones will look upon you any differently because of your afflictions.

Amen.

SIXTY SIX

January 14th, 2024 / late morning

Besides, there are different types of makeovers.

A full makeover doesn't always have to deal with your outward appearance. It can also have to do with a person's *inward* appearance.

Their heart and soul.

A person can be beautiful on the outside, and so cold and ugly on the inside – and vice versa.

In my case, I was so worried about my outward appearance, I had almost forgotten about what *really* mattered. Understandable, yes, but sort of silly nonetheless.

One thing for sure; cancer – and chemo – both will tend to teach you some hard but valuable lessons about your own mortality, and who you *really* are on the *inside*.

Today? I feel like a man who has made a lot of mistakes and paid for all of them ten-fold, which has made me a better man, yet I feel as though I'm still missing something.

Redemption? Maybe. I would like to think God has forgiven me for all of my transgressions and has a place waiting for me in Heaven.

But, I won't know until the day I die, which I would rather not do so soon.

Yes...I think I need to concentrate more on my *inner* being in the future, instead of what some total stranger might think about my outward appearance.

Amen to that.

#

Besides, I have certain plans in place in the future, for my outward appearance.

For example, if I feel like dressing to make myself feel better, I will wear a nice looking Fedora hat, and a black silk scarf. Reason for the hat? Simple enough. It will depend on if my hair actually grows back in, if at all. Why not accessorize my look with a hat to compliment my look?

Add a dark shirt – maybe black or dark blue – and pair of my JC Penney jeans, and...voila!

The *new* David Boyer.

The new man with a new plan.

Amen to that.

Amen to the new outlook, to the new life.

To the new inner me. To the life of faith and hope and possibly a new life altogether, in a better place.

Amen.

SIXTY SEVEN

January 16th, 2024 / late morning

A better place.

I've heard this phrase often in the past, when someone has lost a friend or loved one to cancer.

They are in a better place now.

They are referring to Heaven, of course.

Which for me, brings to mind, what does this better place look like?

Will it be like it is in the movies, or will it be like no other experience a human being has ever imagined in their wildest dreams?

I have been thinking a lot about this phenomenon myself lately, and I hope it is the latter of the two. I'd hate to think that once I passed the pearly gates, all I would have to look forward to is a cheap, Hollywood set piece.

Then again, I'm quite sure our loving God would never treat any of his beloved children that way.

So...what will Heaven *really* be like?

#

I'm going to close my eyes now, and let my imagination take me to where I'd like to be if my own cancer does end up winning the battle I'm fighting right now.

First, as I die, I believe I will see a bright, almost blinding light, as the clouds and Heavens part and the beautiful light of God's own presence shines down on me, as he engulfs me in his loving arms, and escorts me into his Heavenly Kingdom.

Then I will see and hear the faces and voices of all of my friends and loved ones who have passed before me, welcoming me with open arms as well.

Then, I believe I will look down to see an ocean blue body of water, more blue than the sky itself and showing my own reflection, to see that I am young and healthy and handsome, my Heavenly body no longer riddled with the cancer that made my last days on Earth a living hell.

Then, suddenly, I will see the reflections of my past pets, my beloved fur babies, cats and dogs, surrounding me with wagging tails and snuggly purrs and the unconditional love I missed so much after they had passed on.

Passed on to that *better place*.

#

Then, as I lay down in tall, beautiful green grass and fields of multi-colored flowers for a nap – the best and most peaceful nap I've ever had – I will close my eyes and hear music; maybe a love song that reminded me of a girlfriend I lost long ago or my ex wife, and I will smile and no longer be sad at our memories, knowing now that it was just all part of God's plan for me, and them, but we don't know it at the time.

I will hear my favorite music and see flashes of my entire life before my eyes, like a DVD being played on fast forward, but I won't miss a second of how wonderful my life really had been, but hadn't all made any sense until now.

All the heart aches and disappointments.

All of the pain and misery.

All of the times I thought I was all alone, but God had been there the whole time, carrying me.

Yes...it will all make sense then.

My better place.

But for now, I will continue to fight the good fight, because I still have things to do before I leave this world, one of which is finishing this book.

Amen.

SIXTY EIGHT

January 18th, 2024 / early morning

I hate to say this, but I think I need to take a short break from writing for now.

My concentration is off a bit, and I need to find something different to do again, add a little variety to my daily routine. In the past, when I felt this way, doing something different usually made me feel better.

So...until we meet again, take care and may God bless you every day and keep you safe.

Amen.

SIXTY NINE

January 26th, 2024 / early morning

Only three days until chemo again.

Yippee!

Yes, that remark was meant to be sarcastic. It's just that, after being able to eat normally, and without as much pain, I dread going back on my "chemo diet" this soon.

Oh well...it's better than not eating at all.

This time, though, I hope my "after effects" aren't as severe. For some reason, it seems like with each individual treatment, the after effects have grown worse. I don't know if that is normal or not, but I best ask my onocologist to find out.

Other than that, though, I feel half way human – for now, that is.

#

Yeah, I know.

Call me a pessimist and grow weary of my sarcasm, but it comes with the territory.

Speaking of which, something else that comes with the territory is my writing.

As of last week, I started working on a *second* book, based on a real life murder case that took place in Vincennes, in September of 1974.

Several years ago I wrote a book about the case, with my own theory of who had committed the crime, which brought attention to the case for the first time in forty-seven years.

But no definite suspects.

This year, though, a local citizen I know personally spoke up after reading the book, and told me that she thinks she knew who might have committed the crime.

After myself and two of the crime victim's surviving family members examined the new evidence, we have come to the conclusion we now know who the killer really is. My book helped solve a fifty year old murder case! Cool!

Point being, I not only helped to solve the case, but now I have *two* books to work on, more to occupy my time when I feel bad, making those days more bearable.

Once again, what more could I ask for?

Yet another important part of my life that has come full circle now.

Amen.

SEVENTY

January 28th, 2024 / early morning

Twenty-four hours until chemo.

Tomorrow may not be a good day.

I woke up this morning with a runny, bloody nose, a bad cough, and I'm sneezing a lot too. Trouble breathing.

Nope...tomorrow isn't going to be a good day.

But, as usual, I'm hanging in there as best I can, doing a lot of praying and trying to remain hopeful. My *inner* strength, at times, is all I have left, so I must do my best to allow it to take over, and hope for the best.

I hope it's enough.

#

So far, not good.

I could buy some over the counter meds to combat my symptoms – maybe a sinus infection – but my wallet says no. Inflation has even hit the over the counter products now, so I'm just stuck with my symptoms I guess, until further notice.

It seems to never fail for me these days; each time I think my day is going to get better, something happens to make my inner strength weaker, and I don't much left but that to combat my condition.

Yippee.

So...I guess I'll just park my butt in front of the TV, pet my kitty cat, and keep plenty of tissues handy. I have already gone through several boxes of tissues, to soak up this bloody mess, and my sinus passages feel like raw hamburger.

Inner strength, don't fail me now!

#

Chemo is a relentless companion, that's for sure.

I'm beginning to wonder if my hair will ever grow back, my skin will have a normal color again, or my inner body will be able to withstand any more chemo. I've been told I might be able to withstand several radiation treatments, but it could possibly weaken my immune system ever more, and make the bone structure in my face weaken, too.

A feeding tube was also mentioned.

And a colostomy bag.

Nope. I'll pass.

So...I just sit back and watch TV and pet my kitty and hope and pray my day improves.

I hope.

Amen.

SEVENTY ONE

January 28th, 2024 / early morning

Well, needless to say, I had to cancel my chemo infusion for today.

In my current physical condition, I thought it not too wise to push my luck.

But, this also puts me a week behind on my treatments.

Yes, it comes with the territory.

So, I move on, try to find something constructive to do.

It's all I can do.

SEVENTY TWO

February 2nd, 2024 / early morning

Three days until chemo again.

I'm doing my best to stay positive, staying busy and watching some good TV and playing some of my favorite music, etc.

This time, though, there is a big difference in the way I feel; although I'm doing my best to stay positive, at the same time, I am terrified.

I'm afraid that after my next round of chemo, my pet scan will show that I am not in remission, and I still have more treatments to endure – which I'm not sure I'll be able to handle very well.

As it is, I'm weak and sickly any given day, and I'm afraid I will always feel this way, for the rest of my life – however long that may be.

But at the same time, I look forward to the next round of chemo, because I know it helps me.

It's a hard line to walk at any given time. Too many conflicting emotions and feelings going on inside that sickly body that has betrayed you.

Yep...I'm pretty damned scared by it all, and up until now, not much scared me unless it something awfully scary.

And so it goes.

#

So it goes on *every* day.

Today, as I sit contemplating my current situation, all of the negative thoughts suddenly remind me of how important it is to be able to *define* one's self.

But to examine one's human condition – that is, to be able to define one's self – you must first have gone through some terrible life experience, which in my case would be my cancer.

My squamous cell carcinoma.

My constant companion.

It has taught me well.

It has taught me what my real definition is.

For me, my true definition has been one of solitude yet fortitude; one of hopelessness yet of hope; one of despair, yet of optimism.

It has taught me how to survive regardless of whatever obstacles stand in my way.

It has taught me that my *true* definition is one of being a true *survivor.*

Yes, my body has betrayed me.

Yes, my mind is filled with ghastly visions of what may – or may not – come. My heart is heavy and my mood sullen.

I see a *ghost* of my former self each morning in the mirror, yet I see a *survivor.*

I see the NEW me.

I see a man who has been through hell and back and so far, came back relatively unscathed.

I see a man who has a new purpose in life, and that purpose is not one of failure or defeat.

I see a man who has faced death in the face, and is still doing so, without hesitation or fear, regardless of how frightening death seems at the time.

My image may not be all that appealing, but nobody ever said that the possibility of death was a pretty sight.

Yes...I know.

I must sound like a broken record by now.

But, everything I write within these pages is a true story, and written for those who may follow in my own footsteps, although I sincerely hope not.

So, as usual, I move on.

SEVENTY THREE

February 4th, 2024 / early morning

Twenty four hours left until chemo, and I am looking at that same face in the mirror again.

The weak, worn out, ghost face that is now my new identity. The face may look old and pale, but the eyes...still bright and blue and full of life.

Full of *hope*.

The *new* me.

I've often heard that the eyes are the key to one's soul. I don't know about that, but I do know that as I stand staring into my own eyes, I see something I hadn't seen before all of this nightmare began.

I see the *future*.

One that is a bright spot within the darkness, like a beacon within the mist of despair, leading me back home, where I belong.

To *my* future.

One I intend to make the best of, no matter what it takes to do so.

The new *me*.

#

One thing the new me is going to do more often in the future is use my very vivid imagination to it's full potential.

As well as my sense of humor.

For example, lately, the little chemo port I have in my chest, it felt like it was *moving*.

My imagination, of course. I'm sure it's just simple paranoia on my part, after having a foreign object inserted into my body.

An object that may be there *forever.*

So...I use my imagination to come up with a new story. A scary story.

I can see it now...

David awoke with the same pain he'd gone to sleep with, except now it seemed to be worse than ever.

He just knew it had to be an ear infection, an inner ear infection, because of the severity of the pain. It felt as though someone had inserted an icepick into the left side of his chest, and was twisting it back and forth like a corkscrew. It had begun to give him a bad headache as well, magnifying the pain even more.

But the pain wasn't what frightened him the most. What scared him the most was, WHAT was it that was...MOVING around, inside his chest?

He climbed slowly out of bed, noticing that the pain worsened with each and any movement that he made. He stood up, seeing black dots in front of his eyes, feeling dizzy. He shook his head, which hurt but seemed to clear his vision, then walked into the bathroom.

After urinating, he went to the sink to wash his hands. After splashing his face with cold water, he looked up at his reflection in the mirror. What he saw made his blood run cold...

There WAS something moving around inside his chest cavity; and it appeared to be shaped like some type of...tiny CREATURE.

A tiny creature shaped like a...huge insect.

A SPIDER.

David screamed...

See what I mean?

Turning something *negative* into something more *positive*.

Positivity.

And, I can upload my new story to my publishing service as an e-book, and make a few bucks on it down the road.

So...I write!

SEVENTY FOUR

February 5th, 2024 / early morning

Well, today is the day.

Possibly my last chemo treatment, before my pet scan...and, hopefully, *remission*.

Four more days of dry shampoo and sponge baths and a crappy diet.

TV reruns and boring days and restless nights.

But, if it will bring me any closer to the end, to remission, so be it.

Positivity.

Imagination, determination.

So, I move on.

#

Well, at least I have a nice sunny day for chemo.

Sunny with fluffy white clouds and temperatures in the mid 50s. Couldn't ask for a better day.

The lunch menu in the chemo center today is sandwiches and soup or, if you feel brave, some spicy, white chicken chili.

I think I'll have a sandwich. For some reason, chili on top of chemo doesn't sound too appealing; the chemo alone tends to spice up my innards just a tad bit.

But for now, I'll just sit here and look out of the big bay windows and look at the sunshine and listen to the birds singing and watch the squirrels playing on the power lines and close my eyes and pretend I'm somewhere else.

You do what makes you feel better at the time.

#

I wake up about half an hour later to a nurse letting me know it's time to go upstairs to see my main onocologist. To see how my blood work turned out.

It's been pretty good lately, and I'll be keeping my fingers crossed.

As well as indulging in a little hope and prayer, of course.

Wish me luck and add a little prayer to the mix, if you would, please.

#

Well, good news!

My blood work results back. Kidney and liver function looks good.

My lung capacity has risen from 93 % to 99 %. My cholesterol is better. Blood pressure is good. That's good news anyway.

Now, it's lunch time!

Today, I'm having chicken and rice soup and turkey and swiss cheese on wheat bread, with mayo. Yummy!

I think it's very nice of the hospital cafeteria to supply free lunches for the chemo center patients. Along with the food and such a nice, friendly atmosphere supplied by the ladies that work there, and the volunteers who help distribute the food and snacks {yes, even cheese crackers and candy!} it makes the patients there feel so much better.

I would recommend their services any day.

Now...it's chemo infusion time!

Until the next time, my dear readers, you have a good day!

SEVENTY FIVE

February 6th, 2024 / early morning

Well, I'm not feeling too bad, actually.

I know that could change at any given moment, but for now, I'm just going to count my blessings and move on with the day.

I've noticed that since I have decided to try my best to have a more positive outlook toward my life in general, no matter how bad I may feel on any given day, it is much easier to deal with this way.

For example, I've made it a habit to wake up each day and count my blessings:

My brother is here for any extra support.

I have my beautiful, sweet little kitty cat, Holly Jean, who gives me extra snuggles and purrs.

I have my Facebook friends and neighbors who are always sending me well wishes and praying for me.

I have my 37 inch, flatscreen TV for some extra entertainment. I have my music MP3s, to listen to as I lay back in my recliner and close my eyes and allow my favorite music take me away to a better place, to the good old days, way back when, me and my best friends all still alive and healthy and living each and every day like it would last forever.

Most of all, I have me, myself, still alive and kicking and doing my best to stay positive, no matter what life tosses my way each day.

I still have my LIFE.

That, my dear readers, is such a huge blessing in itself, is it not?

I think so.

So...on with the day.

On with my *life.*

Amen.

SEVENTY SIX

February 11th, 2024 / early morning

I am off of chemo now for the next seventeen days.

Thank the Lord.

Over the last few days, I've been doing a lot of soul searching again {imagine that, right?} and I have come to a very odd yet eye opening conclusion.

Cancer *is what it is*.

What I mean is, no matter whether I'm having a good day or a bad day – or in between – my *life* is what it is.

For better or worse.

For richer or poorer.

Just like a strange *marriage* of sorts.

This is *my life*.

I've spent all these months trying to figure out *why* I have ended up here, and the answer was there all along.

Call it fate or destiny or divine intervention or a combination of all three, one thing remains the same.

This is my life, it is what it is, and it's high time to make the best of what's left of it.

It IS what it IS.

Time to move forward, to the next chapter in my journey.

#

Part of my next journey, I'm quite sure, will be finding out *where* my journey will end.

What I mean is, will I still want to keep on writing? Or will I retire from writing?

Will my urge to write just seem to disappear, or will this experience give me even more inspiration to write in the future? Writing has been such a big part of my life for so long, I really can't imagine stopping now, for any reason.

But I really doubt that happens.

But I am quite sure that one thing that's going to happen is, the next story – or book – that I write, is going to be something really *special*, uplifting, instead of dark and grim.

Don't get me wrong, part of my journey, my battle with the Big C, is naturally going to be depressing. It comes with the territory.

My point is, sometimes, whether we like it or not or we think life is so unfair, there are times in our lives when you have to go through hell to find a more Heavenly place.

Which, for me, is *here* and *now*.

The past is now really just *that*; long ago and far away and forgotten.

Now it's time for the *future*.

My *NEW* journey.

One of positive thoughts and special, uplifting tales of a new life and a new attitude and a brand new life ahead, hopefully full of wonderous days and sunshine and blue skies and fields of flowers and endless tales of how much ever the worst of times can bring about something almost magical, fantastical, in my life.

And if my life doesn't turn out that way? No matter. I will just chalk it up to being part of God's plan for me, and accept what blessings I do have, and move on.

You absolutely *have* to appreciate what you *have* been blessed with, before it's too late.

Amen.

SEVENTY SEVEN

February 12th, 2024 / early morning

Yeah...I know.

I'm beginning to sound like a broken record again, right? Maybe so.

But, at the same time, I'm also sounding like a man with a purpose, a man with a *mission*, a mission of...rebirth?

One of spending my remaining days on this wonderful Earth making *good* memories, and leaving behind writings that will hopefully inspire and help others that come after me.

One of leaving something behind for my children and grandchildren and even great grandchildren to enjoy, and hopefully benefit from reading.

A mission of hope and love.

One of...yes, *rebirth*.

#

Let us examine the word; rebirth.

Rebirth – for those of you who may believe in the power of reincarnation – it can mean the act of being born a *second* time, in a whole new body.

Crazy idea, right? Yes, unless it's allowed through divine intervention, which in this case, I don't believe is going to happen any time soon. I'm no Biblical scholar, but I'm not the dullest quill on the porcupine, either.

It can also mean the *revival* of something; such as the renewed interest in turntables and vinyl record albums in the 2000s.

Or...it can mean being "born again," in the eyes of God, reaffirming one's faith in Jesus Christ.

A new *beginning*.

That's where I'm at now; at the very crossroads of a new beginning. My *own* rebirth.

My rebirth will be one of not only renewed faith, but also one of a totally new *path* in my life, one of perpetual sunny days no matter how the darkness tries in vain to steal my light.

I live in darkness, sickness, and fear.

Yet, I wake up each day to bask in the light of my new beginning, chasing my darkness and demons away. It is my rebirth that sets me free from fear and depression and the darkness that seems to surround me like a cloud; dark and thick and oppressive.

It is my rebirth that will keep me alive and thriving, and hopefully help others do the same.

Slowly but surely, I'm starting to feel...*reborn*.

What better gift, what better blessing, could a man in my shoes ask for?

There will be lonely days filled with boredom and irritability. There will be nights filled with sleeplessness and bad dreams.

There will be times I don't even want to climb out of bed to face my day, but with my rebirth, my new light shining down on me, I will somehow make it through those days and be a better man for doing so.

Yeah...I think I'll be just fine.

Amen.

SEVENTY EIGHT

February 14th, 2024 / late morning

Today is my social security day!

I went to Walmart and bought some good stuff to eat and bought my kitty cat some of her favorite treats!

I bought myself another pair of jeans since I've lost so much weight, too. That's another thing I hate almost as much as the pain from the cancer and chemo; having to buy new clothes because my older clothes no longer fit very well. If I wear my older clothes, I look like a baggy old scarecrow. Ha-ha.

But a handsome old scarecrow, right?

Aw...come on, agree with me! I need the extra encouragement!

It's okay. I was just kidding around anyway.

Now, on with my day...

#

Wasn't such a nad day after all.

I got to relax, eat some good food, and just enjoyed my day in general. My kitty cat enjoyed her treats too, and took a nap in my lap, all snuggles and purrs.

It's been a good day.

How good my days may be in the near future may be up for debate, but I will deal with those days as they come along.

First, I am having a C-scan to see how much my chemotherapy has helped me. Then I will have some idea how good my days may be – or not be.

Prayers, please!

SEVENTY NINE

February 24th, 2024 / late morning

Well, I had my C-scan yesterday afternoon, and I haven't seen the results just yet.

I logged into my personal, on line chart for the results, but none have been posted yet.

So now, of course, I have to spend my weekend wondering about it – *worrying* about it, more than anything – and feeling like a nervous wreck.

Remember, it goes with the territory.

Yes, I know.

But, I have already been treading through very dangerous territory already, and it would be nice to feel at least somewhat *hopeful* again.

I will just have to wait and see.

EIGHTY

February 25th, 2024 / late morning

Tomorrow is chemo day again.

Yippee!

Yes, I was being sarcastic.

I can't help but feel sarcastic right now, I guess. I sure would have liked to have seen my test results before I go back on chemo. Who knows? Maybe the results are *not* good, and my onocologist wants to give me the bad news in person.

Which won't make me any difference, of course. Bad news is still bad news, regardless of how it is related to you.

But I hope it's *good* news.

I would like to spend what may very well be my last Spring and Summer *off* of chemo, and free of it's horrible side effects.

I hope so. I really do.

But if not, I will do my best to deal with God's plan for me, and hope it may help others deal with their own cancer journey someday.

Hence this book.

I guess I will find out soon enough.

EIGHTY ONE

February 26th, 2024 / early morning

Well, I got my results yesterday evening.

The swelling in my lymph nodes and the nodule on my right lung are much better, but the cancerous growth on the floor of my mouth is still there.

Not good.

That most likely means even more chemo, and-or some radiation treatments.

Which means my journey has just taken a distinct turn – but in the *opposite* direction.

Not good.

But, surprisingly, I'm not that frightened or sad. I have already told myself that I would accept God's plan for me, so I shall do so.

My feelings might change with time, but I seriously doubt it. Why should I look at it any differently now? That won't change anything.

Whether it be fate or destiny or God's own plan for you, cancer doesn't play favorites, and I doubt that will ever change, either.

#

I've heard recently that we are all *born* with cancer cells in our body, and whether they lay dormant or wake up loaded for bear depends on our own immune system.

In other words, it depends on whether or not we take care of ourselves, live a healthy and righteous life, to lessen our chances of our cancerous "birthright" waking up and eating us alive.

Doesn't sound too fair, does it? I mean, why would God allow innocent children to be born with a possible death sentence? It makes no sense, does it?

Well, that's because we tend to close our eyes to God's plan for all of us, instead of just turning our lives over to him, and let him guide us through our own individual journey.

All of us die from *something* – whether it be cancer or a car accident or gunshot wounds or old age or whatever, nobody stays here forever, it's just the natural order of things.

It's *God's plan*.

It's up to each one of *us* to decide how we may leave this world, and in the meantime, try our best to live a good life, a righteous life, to pave our own way to our Heavenly rewards.

I – all of us – have to keep the faith and trust God's own judgement how we leave here.

Until then? I will keep on fighting the good fight and hoping and praying for the best.

Cancer has *not* beaten me just yet.

#

So, here I am.

In a few hours from now, I will begin another 96 hours of chemo, and, after that, more tests.

And more chemo and more tests.

And probably even *more*.

This was apparently God's plan for me, and I will make the best of it, while I'm still able to do so.

I will wake up each day, glad to be alive, and try to make the best of it.

I will hope and pray and watch beautiful sunsets and wish upon a star and smile at the beauty – and the irony of it all.

In the meantime, I will thank God for each and every day he gives me, despite any pain or discomfort or misery – and be thankful for it.

I will continue to write too, not only because I enjoy it, but also because I hope it will entertain – and help someone else someday.

I've been given a gift by God; why not put it to good use?

For now, dear readers, God bless you all, and I wish you the best on your own journey.

Amen.

David Boyer / February 26th, 2024

The author

David Boyer is a Christian, a multi-genre writer, a true crime buff, and the author of several coming of age novellas, numerous horror and scifi stories, as well as the author of numerous essays including the subjects of government corruption, Christianity, bullying, and cyber-stalking.

He lives in Vincennes, Indiana, with his cat, Holly Jean, who now serves as his copy editor by jumping on the computer keyboard when he's not looking.

210

Books: {Non-fiction}
True crime:
Small Town Murder: True Crime Stories From Knox County, Indiana
Murder In the Hoosier Heartland: Infamous Indiana Murderers & Fledgling Serial Killers
Murder & Mayhem In the Hoosier Heartland: Mysterious Disappearances & Bizarre Murders In Indiana
The Blitz: A Rape Victim's Story
Vanished In Vincennes: the Mysterious Disappearance and Death Of Dolores Oliver
47 Years of Hell: The Dolores Oliver Murder: Still Unsolved
Small Town Murder In Knox County, Indiana: Hate Crimes, Witch Hunts, and A Definitive List of Indiana Serial Killers
The Guy In The Blue Shirt

Non-fiction: {paranormal, bio & memoir}
Haunted Heartland: Haunted Hoosiers Tell Their Ghost Stories
Strange Happenings In the Hoosier Heartland
I Remember When, In Vincennes...Volume 1
Growing Up In Vincennes – Volumes 2 – 5
The Time of Our Lives: Growing Up Cool In Vincennes, Indiana

211

Essays:
Bullying: the Road to Recovery and Forgiveness
Privacy In the Age of the Internet: How Sexting and Sharing Private Photos Can lead To Cyber-Stalking
Once An Alcoholic, Always An Alcoholic? The Cold Hard Truth About Our Addictions
Travesties of Jutice: Flaws In Our Legal System That Imprison the Innocent
Will the REAL Christian Please Stand Up?
Racism in the 21st Century: ALL Lives Matter
Conflicted Souls: How the Man In Black Saved My Life
Crossing the Rainbow Bridge: Saying Goodbye To Our Beloved Pets

Books: {Fiction}
Mystery, Indiana
Human Sawdust
Mutant Moon and Other Stories
Lucid Nightmares – A Collection of Short Fiction
The World According To Luther Biggs

Stories: {Long fiction, novellas}
Mystery, Indiana
The Mind of Luther Biggs
LUTHER
Jenny
Lester Talbot and His Magic Eye
Beautiful Ghosts
Pretty Flamingo
Jack and Norma Jean
The Things We Leave Behind – Volumes 1 – 3

Ghosts of Summer
Gardens
Claustrophobia
The Cemetery Artist
Brain Pie
Beast
The Jailhouse Movie Star
Easy Pickings
The Dominant Thumb
Joyride
The Maverick
Freak
Grandma's Gooseberry Pie
Dancing With the King
Always In My Heart
Hillbilly Moonshine Zombies
Home
Sheva
A Debt Repaid In Full
The Enlightening Darkness
The Good Neighbor
Wander
The Hungry Ones
A Gunfighter's Legacy
Dead Man's Hand
Inhuman Experiments – Part 1, 2, and 3
Jennifer
Spider Bait
Poor Larry
Creepy Crawl
They Call Me The Wolf

Welcome To Deadman's Gulch
Uncle Marty
The Guy In The Blue Shirt
Mutant Moon
Elnora's Eyes
Goodnight, My Love
Wildflowers
Blue Moonlight
Black Midnight
Two Men, Sitting On The Front Porch, Talking About The End Of the World
True Love Never Dies: An Apocalyptic Love Story
Save Me
Shadow Dolls
The Ghosts Of Halloween
Restless Hearts
The King Of Pain

Other recent book releases by David Boyer
{Now available on Lulu.com}

Dolores Oliver, fondly nick-named 'Lert' by her friends as a term of endearment, was out an out-going and friendly woman who was well liked by all who knew her.

Yet, on September 7, 1974, while on a visit to a local bar to chat with friends, she simply vanished without a trace. Foul play was immediately suspected by her family, who knew in their hearts that they could think of absolutely no one who would want to do her any harm.

Yet her lifeless body was found at the end of

October in a bean field by a farmer in Illinois. Lawrence County coroner Dale Nichols was able to make a positive ID through dental records and a ring Mrs Oliver was wearing.

Who would have done such a thing, and why? Hopefully, VANISHED IN VINCENNES will help to finally solve one of the oldest cold cases in Indiana, and bring her family some closure they have sought for so long.

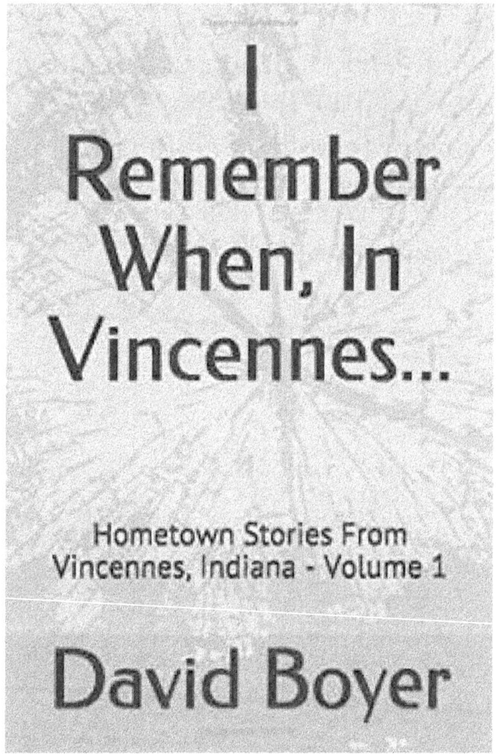

Unfortunately, even small towns – Vincennes included – eventually change, sometimes for the better, and other times, not so much. It's the natural order of things.

Trees grow old and fall. Sidewalks split and crack and are replaced for public safety's sake. Old houses – and all the memories associated with them – are demolished and replaced with parking lots or duplexes. Even historical landmarks, Mother Nature and Father Time having taken their toll, sadly, vanish – except for our own pictures and memories of them.

Luckily for Vincennes residents, local historian Norbert Brown has created a Facebook group page entitled, *Vincennes Remember When*, to help all of us keep our fond memories intact, and to reminisce and enjoy them 24-7.

It was his infinite wisdom of our local history and group page that was the inspiration for this book – and the stories within. Some of these stories may elicit a tear, some laughter.

Some may remind you of an old friend you haven't seen since high school – or, sadly, one that has passed in recent years. Some may remind you of your childhood, your teenage years – or having to bid them farewell, in order to move on to bigger and better things; marriage, children, grandchildren, and a lifetime of wonderful memories that only a tight-knit, loving family can provide.

It is my sincere belief that there will be a story for *everybody* within these pages, regardless of whether you may be a Vincennes history buff or not.

As of 2015, it is believed that there are at least 200 serial killers active in the United States at any given time.

33 of them were from Indiana.

Nobody in their own home town would have wanted to imagine a fledgling {or full fledged} serial killer lurking about, searching for his next victim. Or imagine one being their next door neighbor or the relative of a friend or even attending the local college.

Yet, since the early 1970s, Vincennes, Indiana, Knox County, and Indiana in general has had it's share of cold blooded murder.

It's really sad – as well as terrifying – to even imagine all these brutal, cold blooded murders have taken place in small town communities, where, at one time, we could all trust just about everyone we met at least to the extent they'd do us no harm; a time when could leave our doors unlocked at night or a window open for a cool breeze or not have to worry about where our children were – or if they'd ever come home again.

In SMALL TOWN MURDER, we will be examining local cases, old cases, more recent cases, and the aftermath it leaves behind for the victim's families – as well as taking an in-depth look into a deep, dark, world none of us would ever want to see – but has been here all along, and, most likely, always will be.